This book is dedicated to all Fred Dibnah fans throughout the world..........

Dr. Frederick Dibnah MBE
1938 - 2004

One mistake up here and it's half a day out with the undertaker!

Fred Dibnah
Memories of a Steeplejack

Compiled by: Paul Donoghue.

Design by Dave Oakley
(Pega Print & Design Sheffield)
Project Co-ordinator: Patrick Donoghue
Photographs: The Paul Donoghue Heritage Collection
Additional contributions & photographs:
Sheila Dibnah, Neil Carney, Alf Molyneux, David Jack, Peter Johnson, Stuart Radford, David Hall. Eddie Chatwood. Geoffrey Van Leeuwen. Gordon Connolly. David Banks - Fear. David Devine. The Bolton News, Bury Times and Leigh Journal. Alan McEwan. John Haslam. Gary Burns. Michael Webber. Empics.

Illustrations: Brian Smith
Edited by: Patrick Donoghue.

Produced for Rallyscene and W.H. Smiths.
Website: www.freddibnah.tv
Email: rallyscene@aol.com
Telephone: 01246 811112

Printed by: William Gibbons & Son. Wolverhampton

Copyright: Paul Donoghue
ISBN 978-1-4276-2167-2

This edition published 2007 by Paul Donoghue.

Rallyscene, The Pond House, 59 Rotherham Road Clowne, Derbyshire, S43 4PT

SOME CHAPTERS WERE ORIGINALLY SEEN IN THE DISCONTINUED HARD BACKED BOOK FRED DIBNAH "A MUCH LOVED STEEPLEJACK". THE BOOK HAS NOW BEEN RE-FORMATED AS A WH SMITH EXCLUSIVE (WITH A FREE DVD) MEMORIES OF A STEEPLEJACK.

Contents
Memories of a Steeplejack

Introduction - By Sheila Dibnah - 6

The Book That Never Got Finished - By Fred Dibnah

Mr Smith's Story - 10

Life of a Steeplejack - 18

They Came From the BBC - 23

Fred Wins a BAFTA - 29

The War Effort - 31

Fred and his Land Rovers - 35

What's it like to be Famous - 40

Fred's Chimney - 42

A series of stories written by Fred Dibnah.

Contents
Memories of a Steeplejack

The Early Days - By Michael Webber - 45

Fred Dibnah to Air Traffic Control - By Eddy Chatwood - 55

The Cockermouth Mill Chimney Drop - By Alan McEwen - 57

The Farnworth Chimney Drop - 62

Fred Dibnah visits the Great Dorset Steam Fair - By Paul Donoghue - 65

The Great Canvey Island Chimney Disaster - By Fred & Sheila Dibnah - 70

Always in the Papers - By Sheila Dibnah - 75

A Trip of a Lifetime - By Alf Molyneux - 77

A Date with her Majesty - By Sheila Dibnah - 82

My Time with Fred - By Neil Carney - 86

Doctor Fred - By Sheila Dibnah - 89

Fred's Last Chimney - By Sheila Dibnah - 93

A Big Day in Bolton (Fred's Funeral) - By Paul Donoghue - 99

Moving the Engines - By Michael Webber - 106

Eulogy by Patrick Donoghue - 112

INTRODUCTION
by Sheila Dibnah

A name like Dibnah naturally leaves its mark. I am often asked what it was like being married to 'Our Fred,' but so far no one has asked me to write it down. Until now. I welcome the opportunity to give you, the reader, a snap-shot glimpse into 'Dibnahworld'. Because I was the closest person to Fred during his final years, this book goes further than any previous publication - giving you exactly what you want. The pure, essential Fred Dibnah MBE. The following stories unfold not merely as a collection of reminiscences by close pals and casual aquaintances, "but, by contrast" show exactly what Fred was like in the words of his widow. You'll not be disapointed...

Anyone knows, despite the famous name, I can't mend a steam engine, or ladder a 200ft factory chimney. I'm no expert on the industrial history of the 20th century and I can't draw a detailed and accurate illustration of a cross section of a working mineshaft, but I can tell you about a man who did. That's my particular skill.

'The tall blonde', (as Fred always called me), came into his life in 1996 and things looked up – especially for Fred, who at 5'5" didn't feel the least intimidated or show the slightest concern that some lass from a show business background, towering above him at 5'10", was his new drinking buddy and interested in seeing his mechanical lubricators! It has since been suggested that if you put a thousand people side by side and paired them up, I wouldn't have made the last fifteen. However, none of that mattered, because somehow, Fred and I gradually grew to love each other. I think he also considered me quite mad, because I liked cast iron and had a bit of a fetish about spanners, so that helped to oil the wheels of a love affair with Mr Dibnah!

It was a fantastic life as Mrs Dibnah. The old Chinese proverb 'May You Live In Interesting Times' always springs to mind, when I recall those happy years spent with my famous hubby. The fact he was a celebrity meant Fred was perceived by the public as 'being special' but fame to him was all in a day's work. The grubbier and more dangerous the better, and if the BBC cameraman nearly got killed at the base of some chimney during a drop, it was something to be bragged about in the pub afterwards! All the programmes on telly leave the viewer in no doubt Fred was happiest in his treasured sheds in Bolton, or swinging about on a bosun's chair from a tall chimney.

Paul Donoghue, of independent film production company Rallyscene spent a great deal time with Fred and his second family, filming fly-on-the-wall style during the early 90s and they became firm pals

as a result. This prompted Paul's highly acclaimed tribute film 'Remembering Fred Dibnah', released shortly after Fred's death . With this book comes a free DVD produced by Rallyscene which includes a unique selection of previously unseen footage such as recent filming in the yard, sheds, interviews and the final removal of Fred's treasured engines from Radcliffe Road.

This new, long-awaited book compilation by Paul Donoghue, working with the most comprehensive Dibnah archive in the country, gives some of the zeniths of the steeplejack, steam expert, historian and the person we all came to know as 'Our Fred'. And because Fred always wanted to do a book on the history of steeplejacking – which Paul was also helping him to achieve – his own thoughts, feelings and knowledge will leap up from the pages, bringing to life once more that familiar, unmistakable charisma.

The colourful character of complexities that Fred became not only to a public who adored him, but also to family members and friends means he will never be forgotten. But what can I say about Fred

that hasn't already appeared in print? Well, I can tell you exactly what he was like to live with. How his 'obsessions' with steam, engineering, coal mining and all things mechanical shaped our lives. I can tell you about his love of a pint or two and what he expected from a traditional wife. The trouble is – so can two other Mrs Dibnahs! What they cannot know however, is how illness, and sheer tenacity to get his Aveling & Porter Colonial Steam Tractor finished affected his final years.

My life will never be the same now Fred's gone. But then, all of us feel that way – maybe that is why you have decided to buy this book? He was a good man, my husband. He rightly deserves to be remembered with love and pride and although there can only ever be one of his kind, I just hope these following stories - some of which have never been available before - will prompt his fans and followers to forever remember him and all that he achieved.

So pour yourself a cool pint of Guinness, get comfortable, and tuck in...

Sheila Dibnah

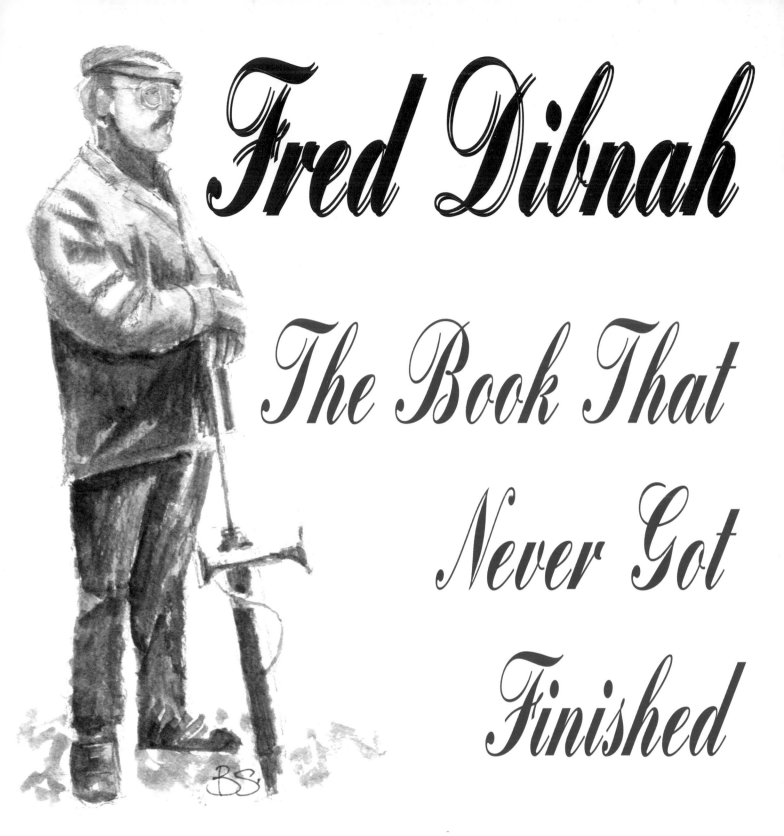

Fred Dibnah

The Book That Never Got Finished

In 1995 Fred Dibnah started to write his life story. Due to Fred's ever increasing fame and television commitments the book was shelved. It is fitting that the first eight chapters in this book are in Fred's own words.

Mr Smith's Story
by Fred Dibnah

Mr Smith, who came to be known as 'The Lancashire Steeplejack', is reckoned to be the man who brought in the standard method of 'laddering' a chimney. He was born in Coventry around 1849, and Joseph Smith was quite young when he came to live in Rochdale, Lancashire. Although he only stood at five feet five and a half inches tall, he seems to have had a striking presence, even though he appears to have been a man of few words. As well, he seems to have been a rather serious sort of chap in some ways and, unlike most steeplejacks, he didn't smoke or drink! I think he must have been a bit of a character though, because he went about the country in a Pullman Coach, and was considered something of a gentleman because he liked to dress in a jacket and tie.

As the Victorian factory owners' empires steadily grew and more chimneys shot up skywards, the owners came to realise that nobody had given much thought on how they were going to maintain those chimneys. They couldn't just close the whole works while somebody went up the inside of the chimney and examined it, because, obviously, this would lose the company vast sums of money from interrupting output.

It seems that Joseph Smith started out as a scaffolder and slowly took up steeplejacking. To all intents and purposes he was very successful and would travel great distances to mend, straighten and fell chimneys, and that's where the Pullman Coach came in. To be mending a chimney in, say, Coventry, (and the business of steeplejacking being controlled by the weather), it was difficult to go into lodgings if you couldn't work for a number of days and then come up against a big accommodation bill. Also, in those days, lodgings were sometimes a bit dodgy, with damp beds, cold and dirty rooms, and rotten food. In those days, (before Environmental Health Departments and the Health and Safety Officer!), to have a caravan and live on the job in nice, cosy and warm conditions – a bit like the fairground men – were much better! So Mr Smith had his own beautiful Pullman wagon purposely built for his own use. It had oriental mirrors, fine furniture, and all the necessary cooking paraphernalia. This was loaded on to a goods train and was pulled to the next town he was working in. The ladders, planks, ropes and other equipment followed on in another coach.

From what I can gather, like many men of his time, Mr Smith lived his life as a fearless, relentless individual who undertook the task in hand with great vigour. He lived in a time when there were a great many chimney disasters, such as the collapse of the Newlands Mill chimney in Bradford on 28th December 1882. There were 54 people killed and many injured; this was caused by some steeplejacks attempting to straighten the thing.

Another disaster occurred at Huddersfield on 18th November 1893 when a chimney was brought down in a gale. The mill owner had instructed an inexperienced steeplejack to heighten the chimney by over thirty feet. Later it was heightened still further, all this without any consideration of the fact that the base was only six feet square. Sure enough, it came tumbling down, killing two men and causing considerable damage to the surrounding properties.

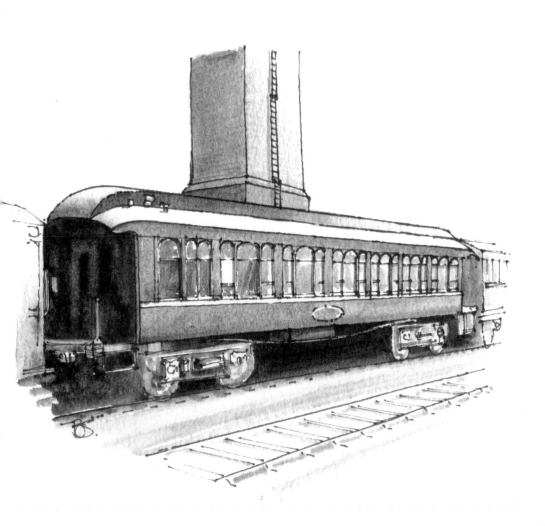

Another calamity tells a similar tale and came to be known as 'The Great Cleckheaton Chimney Disaster'. This stack was at Marsh Mills, Cleckheaton in Yorkshire and was undergoing repairs in 1892 when it collapsed on 24th February, killing 14 people. The stack had been heightened several times and when it got to 180 feet high it got a bit top-heavy for its circular base of about 45 feet diameter. It weighed about 500 tons when the whole thing crashed down for about 70 feet on its haunches, then leaned over and fell down on to the mill and destroyed it.

It is easy to see why Mr Smith had such a good reputation, as there are no records of him causing any disasters or owt like that, or being incompetent in any way. This guy knew what he was doing and so was in much demand. He did have moments of great courage as well, like when he faced unexpected danger. There is a tale of him working at the top of a chimney with an assistant who suddenly went doolally. The pair of them were up on a scaffold at Sutton's Corn Mill, which was near the old railway station in Rochdale. Without any warning the assistant gave out an almighty wail and leapt into space. As the man went over the edge, Mr Smith seized him by the ankle, and the crazed man hung like a dead weight, writhing and shrieking. But Mr Smith put in a superhuman effort and pulled the man up until he was able to seize his belt. Having got a firm hold, Mr Smith managed to pull the poor unfortunate back on to the platform. Even then the drama wasn't over as the man started furiously punching Mr Smith, and there they were, battling it out on a narrow platform 200 feet up in the air. So desperate was the man to do himself in by jumping off, he even tried to free himself by biting Mr Smith, who was to bear the scars from this appalling, violent incident for the rest of his life. But that wasn't the end of the matter. Feeling himself becoming weak from the effort he'd put in, Mr Smith realised that desperate measures were called for if both of them were to stay alive. He managed to grab a small iron crowbar and bopped the madman over the head. Even that was not enough, and a second blow was needed to finally subdue him. Then Mr Smith attached a piece of rope to the man's belt and lowered him safely to the ground. By the time he got there, the peculiar fellow had almost become conscious again. Many people witnessed the extent of the man's madness, including some who said that he was offered a drink from a stone bottle of brandy as a restorative, only for him to bite the neck off the bottle with his teeth! Many witnesses were at Rochdale station waiting for trains and they were totally gob-smacked by what they saw.

I fancy it might all be a bit of an exaggeration, but even if it is, it's still a good tale. Mind you, it might be true, because most steeplejacks are bloody mad anyway!

He managed to grab a small iron crowbar and bopped the madman over the head. ....

Curiously, despite being almost dragged to his death on that occasion, Mr Smith regarded his most perilous adventure as the one where he climbed 265 feet up Rochdale Town Hall. This was done to place a flag on the summit on the anniversary of the birthday of a late statesman. The first part of the climb was nothing untoward in itself, but then he had to shin up a lightning conductor hand over hand. He found the conductor to be in a very unsafe condition, but not being a faint-hearted sort of chap in any way he carried on regardless for his own safety. Having reached the top of the conductor another difficulty awaited him. In those days an antique and fearsome ornament of the figure of Saint George was up there as a substitute for a weathercock. To finish the job, Mr Smith had to climb up on to the shoulders of this thing in order to lash an 18 feet pole to its chest. To the amazement of the crowd below, Mr Smith, wobbling about without much of a foothold, managed the task. The crowd shouted and cheered and the event became part of local history and was talked about for years afterwards. The brave Mr Smith – The Lancashire Steeplejack.

What you have to remember though, is that blokes like him were sometimes admired as much as television personalities are today, because nothing much was happening in people's lives like now. It was a form of entertainment for the people to see a couple of blokes balancing up there on top of a chimney or swinging about on a bosun's chair – it was quite a remarkable sight. The Victorians had a splendid sense of drama as well, so this would be an ideal situation for anyone who was a writer at the time to display their talents to anyone fortunate enough to be able to read. But how far some of these reported tales about Mr Smith go as to being totally accurate, nobody really knows. Like one which reports that he was working at the top of a chimney that was out of plumb by a great degree when he heard a groan and knew that the chimney was about to tumble. He slipped quickly down a lifeline and fled for his life, just as the thing crashed over to the ground within 10 yards of him. I've heard tell of another incident when Mr Smith was removing dangerous coping stones from the top of a factory chimney and one of the stones fell off. It hit the scaffolding, carrying it away from beneath his feet. He managed to throw himself against the very top edge of the chimney, which was the usual nine inches thick. His head and shoulders were hanging over the inside of the chimney, his legs and the rest of his body being over the outside.

Scorched and suffocating from the hot, sulphurous air and smoke, he still managed to work himself round to the ladders on the other side of the chimney, enabling him to reach the ground safely.

I'll tell you in a minute about another one. Now I do find this one very hard to accept as anything like true because, having spent my life around chimneys great and small, I can't believe he fell off one and just walked away! What is certain though is that he possessed a muscular constitution and had the strength of an ox. Although he had an easy-going attitude he planned everything out carefully before starting anything. He had the ability to judge distances and measurements by the eye. Not such a bad way for a bloke working as a steeplejack to be. The story where he was supposed to have fallen off a chimney happened in August 1887. Having safely fixed a lightning conductor on a new steeple at Friarmere Church in Delph he then left to fix a mill chimney at Linfitts. This chimney was about 75 feet high and, as usual, he had fixed the ladders one above the other, much the same as I do today. But while fixing the last section on this occasion it collapsed and the ladder fell to the ground with him on it. Carried into a nearby cottage by onlookers, they were amazed to find that he was still alive. A doctor rushed to the scene shortly afterwards and was reputedly astonished to find that not only was Mr Smith still alive but in fact he had no broken bones, only a few bad bruises. A little while later Mr Smith was able to walk unaided to a waiting cab. I've got a copy of an old book written about him in 1898 which ends this story by saying "Mr Smith was none the worse for his tremendous fall". Some guy, eh? Bu-boom!

But not only did Mr Smith undertake alteration and restoration work but naturally he felled chimneys too. In fact, one of the first sets of pictures ever taken of a chimney felling was of his felling one just outside Walsden Railway Station in Lancashire. Mr Smith had been commissioned to undertake this work by the Lancashire and Yorkshire Railway Company. The chimney was made of stone, stood about 135 feet, and weighed about 400 hundred tons, so it wasn't a very big one. By comparison, the greatest chimney he felled was an octagonal one at Higher Broughton, Manchester. The stack was 270 feet high, 92 feet in circumference and seven feet eight inches thick at the base. They reckoned it contained one million bricks and weighed about 4,000 tons. Because of it being such a big one, it took Mr Smith and five of his men a full eight days to cut away the base and underpin it with 130 props. One problem he faced about bringing this big bugger down was that it leaned in the opposite direction from which they wanted it to fall. By all accounts, Mr Smith did a grand job and was complimented on his underpinning technique by Sir Leader Williams, the engineer for the Manchester Ship Canal who witnessed it, along with another twenty thousand spectators on the day!

A very dangerous thing to do is straightening a very tall chimney that is leaning or 'out of plumb'. I've done this myself and it needs very careful planning and skilful attention for the operation to be a success. One in particular that Mr Smith attempted is mentioned in the little book that I have about him and it's worth repeating. A round stack measuring nearly 200 feet was no less than four feet six inches out of plumb. The method he used goes like this: in order to straighten it, he cut out a course of brickwork from the convex side with chisels. Then a series of

iron wedges varying in size from about three feet to six inches were temporarily substituted for the course of bricks. It was when this was complete that the real tricky stuff came about.

Certainly a character, Joseph Ball always wore a tightly-fitting black suit, the trousers exceedingly short and almost too tight....

The smaller wedges were withdrawn first, followed by the larger, the gaps being filled with a thinner course of bricks and mortar. So, as the wedges were

taken out the stack gradually returned to the perpendicular by the force of gravity and it was finally brought back to a true plumb line. It goes without saying really but it's a very delicate operation and extremely dangerous. Just that little too much violence or too much brickwork removed and then – WHAM! – the whole structure would become unstable and topple over. Experience shows that in most cases a single cut would be enough to straighten a chimney, but occasionally it is necessary to make as many as four. The stack I mention here that Mr Smith worked on needed three such cuts before it was straight again..

However, without a doubt the things he is most likely to be remembered for today are his laddering techniques, which are still in use today. 'The Lancashire Way' is a bit different from how the Yorkshire steeplejacks would ladder a chimney as their ladders stand away from the chimney wall and it is their way that I have always done my chimneys. Good bloke, that Mr Smith – I would have liked to have met him.

Another bloke I would have liked to have met was Joseph Ball of Oldham, who was apparently a bit mad. He was a charismatic, eccentric man who started out as a chimney sweep, later becoming a steeplejack. He had ideas of grandeur and eventually went on to build his own castle in the middle of a row of terraced houses! By all accounts, he had a charming, persuasive manner and, despite being very intelligent, was totally illiterate, never getting beyond signing his own name. Not only that, he would speak at times in a nonsensical way, misusing and jumbling words around, punctuating his sentences by throwing in big words and similes, resorting to sarcasm when he felt the need arose. In spite of these liberties he took with the Queen's English and his odd quirks it was easy to gather his meaning, and he became very successful in business.

Certainly a character, Joseph Ball always wore a tightly-fitting black suit, the trousers exceedingly short and almost too tight. He also wore large, coffin-like boots, a white shirt-front with a two and a half inch 'stand-up' collar without a tie, and a black bowler hat. Perhaps Laurel and Hardy managed to get some inspiration from his description. That would have

pleased him no end because he also moved in theatrical circles as well as being a steeplejack.

Working as a chimney sweep as a young boy, his paradise on earth was the glittering lure of the music halls. His mind was captivated by painted ladies of dubious repute swinging their limbs about for all to see. This attraction prevailed for all his life and was to have great influence on him in his later years. But his canny business mind, sense of the theatrical and the almost naturally instinctive way he had of relating to people brought him a fair bit of reward in the steeplejacking job. Once, for instance, when he had to visit Lord Salisbury at Hadfield House on a business matter, it was typical of him to seize the moment. As they stood at the front of the mansion, Mr Ball suddenly scrambled up the gutter downspout to prove a point, frightening the poor Marquis almost to death. No doubt he got the job under discussion!

These men were my steeplejacking heroes when I was a kid and I once went to see where Joe Ball is buried in Oldham Cemetery. Funny that – I would have thought the poor bugger would have died with his boots on at the top of some chimney, but he didn't! Ah well...

Working as a chimney sweep as a young boy, his paradise on earth was the glittering lure of the music halls....

Life of a Steeplejack

Transcribed from a Fred Dibnah talk

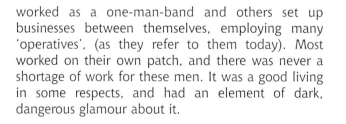

Imagine it! You're stuck on the top of a two–hundred–and–odd–foot factory chimney. It is winter, frosty, blowing a gale, and starting to rain; you can feel the damned thing swaying in the wind. It's taken a fair bit of effort to get up here in this filthy weather, but somehow you manage to concentrate on the task of doing repairs and mending the thing until it's time to go down for a butty and a couple of pints at dinnertime.

All my life I've known what sheer hard effort this game is. Yet, I enjoy it. Especially on a nice, warm, sunny day, swinging about on my bosun's chair with a paintbrush; or doing a bit of pointing with my trowel. Up here, you are your own boss. You can ponder on what you have to do next on your steam engine back home, and watch life go peacefully by. Yeah, I loved days like that. Definitely!

A lot of folk don't seem to appreciate that in the past, there were dozens and dozens of blokes doing this same job, week in – year out. Some steeplejacks worked as a one-man-band and others set up businesses between themselves, employing many 'operatives', (as they refer to them today). Most worked on their own patch, and there was never a shortage of work for these men. It was a good living in some respects, and had an element of dark, dangerous glamour about it.

From about 1700 to 1800, industrial chimneys were usually square and not very tall, perhaps no more than about 30ft high, and were built as part of the engine house. Then along came Mr. James Watt with his first steam engines in 1776. The boilers for these needed much stronger draught, so larger free-standing chimneys had to be built to create this effect and were connected to the boiler by flues. With taller chimneys, the base had to be much thicker to deal with the increased weight of stone or brickwork. It wasn't necessary to take this up the full height of the stack, so they had a characteristic tapering appearance called 'the batter' as the walls got thinner and thinner towards the top.

But it wasn't until the first part of the 19th century and the grand mechanisation of the cotton industry with steam power that wealthy industrialists needed to build even bigger, better and taller chimneys. These gradually became more ornate, sporting fancy tops and brickwork all cleverly designed, so they reflected the owners' money and status in society, as well as being functional.

The mill chimney, by nature of the way it worked, had to be designed by specialists in the field, and such men were called 'factory engineers' in Lancashire. The many aspects of chimney-building needed a well-educated man with a brain to be able to calculate wind pressures in relation to the height, weight, diameter and the form of construction. They used graphics to work this out, and would consider the materials to be used in connection with the nature of the industry that the firm was involved in as well. Also, a lot of guesswork was done – as they all came to different conclusions, and couldn't reach an agreement about it.

Once a design had been agreed upon, specialist chimney-builders then undertook the construction. Considering the amount of work involved, it is pretty amazing to think that, for example, Blinkhorn's large chimney in Bolton, which stood at no less than 369ft 6ins, was built within sixteen weeks from the word 'go'.

At the turn of the century, it was quite common to cut the first sod, build a cotton mill, and have it spinning cotton within twelve months. That meant they would build a five-storey-high mill, equip it with about four Lancashire boilers, a two-hundred-foot chimney, and a steam engine, and all in less than a year!

However for the chimney, after the foundation had been established, if it was a circular one, (which was the easiest to build), the rest of the job was fairly simple. The octagonal or square chimneys tended to be older ones built around about the 1890s and 1900s. In Lancashire cotton districts, they had a tendency to build these. It is amazing, that because local chimney-building specialists built them all, from town to town they were different. For instance, around Preston, there were heck of a lot of square ones – and in Bolton; they tended to be octagonal. Later on, by 1910, they were building round ones nearly everywhere.

A lot of folk don't seem to appreciate that in the past, there were dozens of blokes doing this same job, week in - year out.

When they started on the foundation, they had a block of wood, a piece of string, and a six-inch nail. If it was a circular chimney, one man held the block of wood in the middle of the foundation, and the other guy holding the string, (which was roughly half the diameter of the basement course), wandered round with the nail, closely followed by the foreman bricklayer. He laid an outside course of bricks in circular form, all the way round. Then they would do the same again, with another course about four feet inside the first. Then they spread the semi-liquid mortar with a paddle like a garden hoe, in the gap. They put the bricks in dry; they didn't lay them with a trowel, one bed at a time, all the way round. Then

the next outside course went up, then the same thing again, but an inch stepped in. Liquid mortar again, which ran between the head joints of the brickwork underneath, and then more dry bricks. They carried on doing this, and gradually, it's coming up like a pyramid. What you ended up with is practically a solid mass – no air holes or 'owt.

You could stand on it easily, but as it got gradually thinner going up, they started leaving four bricks out on the inside course and put two putlogs across, (that's two pieces of wood), and a decking made of tongue-and-groove boards, with a trapdoor in the middle, like in a windmill. So if anybody dropped a brick it meant the poor bloke at the bottom loading the bricks in the tub, didn't get one on his head!

Large factory chimneys were always constructed like this – working up from the inside, without the use of any scaffolding, moving the wooden platform up as required. As the chimney got higher, about every six feet or so, they left out another four bricks, and put another two putlogs across and then built another platform, by moving the last one up. There are a lot of variations on this method, though, basically, it is the same. Sometimes, about every thirty feet, they would leave bricks out. That means they would put the first platform up, and when they got six feet up,

they would just erect four thirty-feet tall poles, and lash two pieces of timber across, and place another wooden deck on there. It couldn't fall over, because it was trapped inside the brickwork. Roughly every fifteen to twenty feet, the brickwork steps in half a brick. So if it started off, say, ten bricks thick on the bottom, twenty-odd feet up it went to nine bricks. Then eight bricks, then seven, and then six! Right up to the top, until the wall ended up about nine inches thick.

And even though many were only this wide at the top, almost the thickness of a garden wall, some of them had stonework on, which reached out into space for about five feet! How the hell did they balance that on top of a great chimney? It never ceases to amaze me, how they must have struggled getting them on. There is no way it could have been done easily. The other thing – the ones that were built at the turn of the century, especially in areas like Lancashire, had terracotta tops. Beautiful, bright-red, fancy moulded tops. These were all hollow segmental pieces, and even though they were about six feet long, and two feet across once you had them into position on the top of a chimney, they were filled in with concrete to give then strength. It created one solid lump of what looked like bright-red brick.

When there were four big boilers in action at the bottom, that chimney never went cold as long as the mill was in business, so they were impervious to the weather. But later, when boilers became more economical, and later still when bad times came and the mill shut down, it was terrible news for terracotta-topped chimneys. Because the damp got in and they froze, which cracked them apart. The sulphur content of the coal smashed and expanded them, which meant great lumps would tumble down; so most of the terracotta ones have now been destroyed.

So you see, although folk remember me for being on telly as a steeplejack and knocking chimneys down, not many wonder about those poor blokes who had to build them in the old days.

So you see, although folk remember me for being on telly as a steeplejack and knocking chimneys down, not many wonder about those poor blokes who had to build them in the old days.

Donald Paiton

The late Donald Paiton came to work for Fred in the 1970s. Donald was in his 60s but was still as strong as an ox. He was known by Fred as 'his man at the bottom' and complemented Fred with his building skills and his dry, sardonic sense of humour. He was grammar-school educated and had a sharp mind. They did many jobs together and Donald can be seen in all of Fred's early BBC documentaries. Donald was a teetotaller and managed to keep Fred in check with his lunchtime drinking habits. Fred had been known (if the mood took him) to spend the whole afternoon in the pub.

Donald's classic line

A passer by once said, seeing Fred at the top of a chimney, "Has he ever fallen off?" "Yes", said Donald, "Only the once, but I caught him."

They came from the BBC
By Fred Dibnah

I had in my opinion reached the peak of my career –
I'd got a job mending the Town Hall clock in Bolton,
which is the biggest building in the town! I'd made 16
stone pillars for the balustrade around the top of the
lantern, and the job was going well.

One day the public relations man from the Bolton
Council appeared and said, "Next Thursday, 'Look
North West' are coming to see you about going on
the news", and I thought, "God, that's television!"
and if you've never been on telly and you're
somebody like me, it's a scary sort of thing.

Thursday morning came and me and Donald were up
in the lantern, 200 foot up in the sky. A grey van
arrives on the precinct down below, with the words
BBC on the side. These fellers got out, put the tripod
up and put the howitzer on, as I call it.

*.......... I thought God that's television, and if you've never been on
tele and you're somebody like me it's a scary sort of thing ....*

The man who's coming to do the interview has the reputation of being a mountaineer and a rock climber, so I thought this will be a really good interview because he won't be afraid of walking on a bloody plank 200 foot in the sky if he's a mountaineer, will he?

To get to where I'm working they have to use a lift for two storeys, then it's 'Shanks's pony' up wooden staircases through the clock and the bell frame, up high ladders inside the big lead dome and eventually you end up in the lantern 200 and odd foot up. The mountaineer appeared at one of the orifices, one of the holes out of the side, (there were eight ways out).

The presenter/mountaineer arrives where I am, he's got his microphone with a wire hanging out of it, and he's got his board with all his questions on. I looked at him and said, "Are you coming out on the woodwork to do the interview here?" He said, "Piss off, no way, I'm staying in here".

From where I am, I look 200 foot down below at all the little people running about like cockroaches on the precinct.

He did the interview from inside, with me outside, you know, shoving the microphone through the hole to talk to me. The interview went well and I must confess to looking forward to seeing myself on the telly.

You know they always put the idiots on last on the news in case it's all been bad news. Men who think they can fly or men who think they've invented perpetual motion and it's to give you a bit of a laugh in case it's all been miserable bad news, you see. Well they put me on at the end of the last three minutes. I enjoyed watching myself on telly and was very popular for a while; everyone in my area had watched me.

A few days later the phone rang, it was a man from the BBC. "Can I come and see you with a television director?" I said, "Yes if you want". I'm an easy-going sort of guy like, you know.

Next day he arrived. When I saw him I thought 'Bloody hell, he looks just like Stewart Grainger!' He was six foot tall, all dressed in denim, with a cap with the biggest neb I've ever seen in my life, you know, before they became popular in England, you know one of them big 'uns with a hole in the back, all the kids have got them now. He also had a pair of boots like two canal boats and he talked in a different language; I didn't understand what he was on about, but we ended up down the pub. I'll never forget the

Anyway, I said, "Well I think we should put the ladders up" and he said, "How do you do it", and I said, "Well, verbally it's very complicated, but I'll show you." So I set off and we got one and a half ladders up a chimney stack and he said, "Forget it, it's too technical. They'll get bored and turn off, you know". He says, "We'll bob over next week and see if it's worth it, Jean." And they went away with a real nonchalant manner.

Anyway, all week I got to thinking about this and I thought, 'I'm going to keep shoving the ladder business and portray how steeplejacks put ladders up the side of a 200 foot pile of bricks with nothing there, only a smooth wall,' you see.

Next week came. He was just as adamant, and he didn't want to know about me laddering a chimney. At the end of the evening but for the grace of God it nearly never happened but he muttered something like, "Where are you working?", and I said, "Shore, near Oldham", which is a little village on the mountains on the outside of the town.

next bit, at the end of the evening I said to him, "What do you want me to do? Give you a ring if we're going to do something particularly dangerous or exciting?" and he said, "No don't ring us, we'll ring you", like the proverbial out-of-work actor sort of thing.

But being a bit slow like, I realised that he obviously thought that it was a waste of money trying to make a film about a bloody idiot like me.

Anyway he went; normality had nearly come back into my life and people had stopped saying, "I saw you on the news last Thursday" and all that. Then the phone rang again and this lady came on and said, "I work for the BBC, Can we bob over and see you?", and I said, "Aye of course you can".

The woman arrived and brought her boyfriend who was the director; he was just the same as the other fella but a smaller version, the neb on his cap weren't as big and his boots weren't as big, but he was just as bloody awkward and weird.

By this time I'd had about a month to think about what I would do if they made a film about steeplejacking. The obvious thing to me was that at least they'd want to show me putting the ladders up a chimney from start to finish.

They made this film and it was supposed to be a 20 minute film that he was going to put on the end of a film called 'Earning a Bob or Two', a series about people like vicars who had a sideline and doctors who did something else and fire brigade and policemen and all that.

The series came and went, they gave me 350 quid, but they just kept coming back and having another go, and said, "We'll see you next Wednesday", and "We'll see you in August on the 23rd ." You know, I've even forgotten when they bloody came.

The films won academy awards and they came back and made another four, then they made another five. What I will tell you is that when the BBC came all those years ago, the director had a mini with the arse hanging out of it, but when he went away, many years later, he'd got a brand new bloody Porsche. It's true! And here I am still driving me clapped-out Land Rover!

It was a particularly beautiful area. It had two great big Accrington-brick spinning mills 6 storeys high, with a 90 foot gap down the middle and a 245 foot chimney with a big top on in the middle and five of my platforms underneath the top, and a railway line. Everything was there, all the ingredients for a good Lowry painting.

The series came and went, they gave me 350 quid, but they just kept coming back and having another go, and said we'll see you next Wednesday ....

The backcloth was the bloody Pennine Chain with the sheep farms and the dry stone walls and I'd just got to the top and had a fag and just finished coughing and all that when in they came, round the corner in this mini with the arse hanging out of it. They get out; I'm not going down 245 bloody foot when I've just got to the top so I get on with me job. Ten minutes go by and I look down; he's jumping up and down waving his hands about so I thought, "Well, I'd better go down and see what he wants."

Anyway, I go down and oh! he's inspired and says, "Wonderful, wonderful, we'll be here in the morning". And that is how it all started.

From the Dibnah Archive

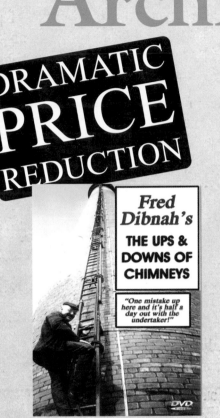
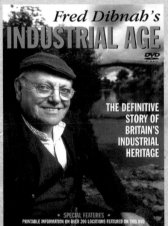

The British Academy of Film and Television Arts

By Fred Dibnah

It was a bit strange really, because Don Howarth's first series about me was shown on BBC2 in the late 1970s, think it were 1978 or summat. Then, within a week or two, they repeated it on BBC1. I'll never forget the night I first got wind of the Award – it was a Friday and it was my turn to go out for the fish and chips. I thought I'd just call in the Conservative Club and have a quick pint on the way. So, I went in and I'm leaning on the bar having a chat with a mate of mine, who was very generous and bought me a pint. Another chap comes over, and he goes "Do you know, you're up for the Academy Awards, Fred?"

I thought to myself, bloody hell, this feller is taking the mickey, this lad's having a bit of a laugh - but he insisted it was true; he'd read it in a showbiz journal or whatever. I said I'd never heard of it, but he goes: "There's three documentaries nominated and yours- 'Fred Dibnah Steeplejack' - is up for one of the Awards".

Then, on the evening of the Awards ceremony, the phone rang, and a very cultured lady from BBC Oxford Road in Manchester said "I don't know if anyone has told you, Fred, but you've been nominated for a BAFTA Award this evening. And even if you do not win, it is a high honour to be selected from the many hundreds. You are in the top three".

So, me and Alison sat there at 8.30pm in front of the television and the usual beautiful skinny actress in long black dress with the brown envelope stood in front of the microphone. After her telling us about the other two up for it as well as ours, she ripped the top off the brown paper envelope and says:

"The winner is – 'Fred Dibnah Steeplejack'!"

We'd won! WON! Bloody hell, I just could not BELIEVE IT!

I'm now watching the box, looking for Mr Howarth, expecting him to spring up at any moment out of the crowd where they're all sat, with the BBC white wine, frilly shirts and stiff collars. Then they announced "Don Howarth Director"

… But he wasn't there! He was in Portugal having a weekend away or summat. They had to give it to someone else on his behalf. But in a few days after he'd got wind of this, he were back again to see me about making some more programmes. One thing I will say about Don – he knew when he was onto a good thing!

The War Effort
By Fred Dibnah

Fred's 1927 350cc AJS

"Um, yeah, me old motor bike, eh?" said Fred. "Well, I had to sell it for the war effort when I had me first divorce, yer see. It's one of the things I regret most is that, 'avin to let me motorbike go. A beautiful 1927 350cc AJS. I once strapped a bloody great anvil on me back, and rode to me mam's house through the streets of Bolton, wobbling all over the place under the weight of it. Some bloke had sold me the anvil for a fiver, and I didn't have a motor car to shift it with. I was just getting an unbelievable interest in starting up me blacksmithing around then, and this thing turned up. Aye, I loved that bike... women though; I mean - they cost a lot of pennies them divorces, don't they?"

Without further ado, he kick-started the machine and immediately shot off across the field in the direction of the arena. For several minutes he gunned the throttle, gathering speed and amusing the crowds with his antics - losing his trade-mark flat cap in the process! He returned exhilarated, obviously having enjoyed the experience. Bearing in mind the catch-phrase that we all had heard so often it was perhaps inevitable that some bright spark shouted out "Did you like that, Fred?" As he dismounted the machine, he swore he would buy another one day, adding, "Its magic, they aren't like modern motor cars these y'know, you can work on 'em and 'av a bit of fun, get about a bit... do you wanna sell it mate?"

The 'war effort' was Fred's divorce from his first wife, Alison, and the bike had been sold at Sotheby's in October 1985, for £1700. Twenty years later it was still a sore point with Fred, who, having been looking at vintage motorbikes at some rally or other, (often after a pint or two!), would go into making vows about how he would buy another one some day. It wasn't anything to do with possessions, just the pure joy and beauty of the machine. To the mechanically-minded Fred, it was like having a bereavement in the family to have to have to part with his treasured bike, and, knowing this, like-minded males would often commiserate. Fred did not have a similar attitude for modern vehicles though. "Me missus has just bought a new shiny car and 'av just dinted the door on the way t'chippy, like. Got into a fair bit of trouble for that, but it doesn't bother me a lot. I've got me lanny, (the Land Rover) that's alreight, a proper vehicle, you can do a lot of bangin' about wi' them, and easily mend owt that goes wrong... but these modern things, well, it's all timing belts and bloody on-board computers or summat. I might buy another motor bike one day. I'm not knackered yet, I could still ride one an' all..."

Age did not matter to Fred. Always young at heart, he had just turned 60 years of age when, (with the owner's permission), he jumped on to a vintage motor bike at a steam rally during one summer.

The facts

Historical Data

Fred's AJS was originally bought (second-hand) by Derek Rosco for £5 from a Scottish church minister called Duncan McClachlan. Derek had spotted the bike for sale in the advertising section of 'Motor Sport' magazine. The bike was later purchased by Fred (after much haggling) for 21 guineas.

The engine shed at Fred's yard that houses his steam engine, Caroline, was originally purpose-built for Fred's motorbike. The windows were constructed so that he could see his pride and joy as he walked past.

'Fred's bike' sold at auction at Sotheby's in October, 1985 for £1700.

P.S. The more 'eagle-eyed' among you will have noticed that the same bike has two different number plates in the photos. Why? - because Fred bought an, (ahem!), dodgy log book for a 250cc machine from a friend. By swapping the number plates Fred could then ride the 350cc bike without having to take a motorbike test. Needless to say, he never got caught!

A Steeplejack's Dream

The Most Famous Land Rover in The World

By Fred Dibnah

One of the most famous Land Rovers in the world

.... Like, really, I've never owned a motor vehicle. Well, I have I suppose, I once owned a 1927 Rover. But it were no good; everything was wrong with it – the back axle was goosed, and the engine block were cracked – and it had various other faults. Well, I really wanted a steam engine anyway, so I flogged it!

Anyway, the first thing I ever had with four wheels was an ex-WD Land Rover. I paid £425 for it – and it was taxed and insured, ready for the road. And it was all painted up nice and green, and had been done up by a good man, who to this day, still specialises in rejuvenated ex-WD.

That one lasted me for a long time. It was rather strange, because it was about five or six years earlier when I passed my driving test – and I'd never since been behind the wheel of anything. I went for this thing, and I'd got to drive it home, which was quite a hairy experience. My driving skills have not really improved a lot, actually!

The thing is - life went by, of course. My idea of maintenance of motor vehicles is nil! I just treated it as a tool. Got out of bed in a morning, pressed the button and it went 'whooomph' – and off it went! The first ailments, like flat batteries, and things like that, and broken half-shafts with putting too much weight on it – expecting too much over what the thing was designed for – crippled it in the end; it was the excessive weight that I put on it. All the time, I'm struggling hard to earn a living, with the steeplejacking, and I could never aspire to a brand-new one.

What always used to upset me immensely was seeing a brand-new Land Rover with a woman in it – handbag on the seat – and that were it! Somebody told me a tale quite recently, about going down the road with a trailer on the back of their vehicle, and being met by somebody – a lady – with a four-wheel drive Land Rover. She refused to leave the road because of the muck at the side of the road – and she was driving a bloody vehicle designed for ploughing across fields!

The thing is - the first Land Rover; I had many traumas – I remember coming back home one day, down the drive, which is quite steep. I put the brakes on – nothing happened. I grabbed hold of the hand-brake – nothing! It carried on proceeding down the hill, through a holly bush, and finally came to rest on the lawn in the middle of the garden. It had the half-shaft sticking out, with a wheel on the end of it! That was disaster number one!

The other frightening thing was - I went to see one of my friends who lived in the country. On the way back, there was an unbelievable rattling which started up. I got home, came down the drive again, and swung the thing round the ash tree at the bottom. I put the brakes on, and the front right-hand corner proceeded to collapse on to the floor! All the wheel nuts had pulled through the hub at the centre of the wheel. Bloody wheel fell off! Anyway, that was the end of that.

The last and final straw with the Land Rover – I came steaming in again, put the brakes on – a big cloud of cream smoke came from under the bonnet. I lifted the bonnet, and the whole electrical system was glowing red…and it bursts into flames…it never went again after that!

So, by this time I had succumbed to a lightweight version. The finances were slightly better by now and I had it painted in 'Holland's Meat Pie' colours. It was dark green at the bottom, and a red, seven-inch wide strip down the middle, and then dark brown at the top. And splendid gold lettering on it: 'F. Dibnah, Steeplejack'. It looked really beautiful; but it was a bit of hard work getting the ladders on the top of it. The other thing – they tell me, these Land Rover men – that these lightweight things were never as well-designed as the ordinary ones, because they were designed for dropping out of aeroplanes. Even though this machine looked very well, I think they'd dropped it out of one-too-many aeroplanes, because it were never any bloody good! Finally, the chassis broke in half, and I sold it for a hundred quid.

Then I got one that I thought would last me through until my retirement, which I'm just now three years short of. Here again, the maintenance aspect of it weren't up to much. I put the petrol in, the oil in and water in the radiator. I did some fairly big jobs with that. I mended two steam engines. I dismantled the steam engines, and brought them long distances. Of course, when you load a Land Rover up, it decimates the steering gear. Coming down the motorway, with the front end drifting across the road makes it very difficult to control. This happens when you're grossly overloaded at the arse-end, you know - the spring's the other way up! Anyway, this went on, then the rust starts and you need another patch on the chassis, then another. Then the bulkhead rotted away.

But then – an unbelievable stroke of luck! A man called Chris Crane rang up from a company called RPI Engineering, in Norfolk. He's seen it on the telly programmes, racing reputedly from one end of England to the other. We only went about a few hundred yards away from home, and rode up and down the motorway a million times, with the camera in all sorts of positions – and up over the moors. We broke the shock absorbers on the T.V. director's car - but it didn't do any harm to the Land Rover - it ploughed on over all this rough tract up near the T.V. mast on top of Winter Hill! It was supposed to be over Dartmoor or somewhere on the series.

Anyway, Chris had seen it on telly. He said, "If you let me convert your Land Rover to gas, I'll do it for nothing!" I said, "Hang on mate, you know, this bloody vehicle is something else - when you're going along the road in the pouring rain and you go through a puddle, you've got to have your wellies on; there's no bottom in it, like!" The engine's goosed, the gearbox is knackered – and I only had one windscreen wiper. The other one, I'd converted it to 'handraulic' – I had a lever inside the cab that you worked. In heavy showers, you'd got to get hold of this handle, and pull it. It was like the very earliest form of windscreen wiper. It was easier than trying to find one that worked.

Anyway, he was bent on doing this job, and kept ringing up about it. I tried to put him off, but finally, I succumbed to his request. One Sunday, the man arrived in a more-or-less brand-new Land Rover, gas-fired, closely followed by John Bolt, a writer from one of the Land Rover magazines. He arrived in a brand-new light-blue Land Rover - hammer-finish – gas-fired. It had all these things that I dream about! Soon after, another man turned up, driving a long-wheelbase ex-WD one, with a rag roof. Three Land Rovers, and my clapped-out one!

.....The engine's goosed, the gearbox is knackered and I only had one windscreen wiper. The other one, I'd converted it to handraulic. I had a lever inside the cab that you worked.....

..... Do you think it will make it, back to Norfolk?...

I said, Well, if I were driving it; yeah, yeah, but I wouldn't go above fifty-odd mile an hour ....

Chris surveyed it – it didn't look too bad – but you couldn't really see underneath. When you looked at the bulkhead, and the rot, the hinges just about holding on to the side, various other things, like bent bumpers and bad bumps in it, where things had hit it on demolition sites – all of that. It's had a few bricks land on it, on odd occasions!

He said, "Do you think it will make it, back to Norfolk?" I said, "Well, if I were driving it; yeah, yeah – but I wouldn't go above fifty-odd mile an hour. At that speed, its O.K. Might be a bit noisy, smoky and uncomfortable, but it won't give up. It keeps going."

So he hung about for about two hours and finally decided he'd have a go at driving it back to Norfolk. He bid us 'good day', and set off. My day wore on in the back yard. Being a bit deaf, I have the bell off a fire engine in my workshop, with a string to the back kitchen. About half-past seven, my wife, Sheila, pulled the string, and rung the bell. When I appeared out of the shed door, she said: "The man from Norfolk's just been on." "What did he say?" "Well, I went "Do you want a word with Fred?", and he carried on, "No, I feel ill and I'm knackered. All the noise and the smoke – I need to rest – I just thought I'd let you know it made it here, tell him I'll ring him next week!""

So next week came, and, about Thursday, the telephone rang. It was Chris. He said, "Well, I've got some bad news – the engine is no good. It's not worth repairing. I'm going to put you a V8 in instead." I thought – bloody hell! I knew it was too good to be true; I knew it would cost me summat! He said "Oh no, I said I'll do it – it won't cost you owt".

Months and months went by, and by this time filming had started for the new series, 'Magnificent Monuments', (more about that later). The director wanted the vehicle back to do some of the shots, but we hadn't got it!

On one occasion whilst filming, we were up in Edinburgh Castle. This old Darby and Joan couple came up to me, "Oh – hello, its Fred isn't it!" They went on "They've got your Land Rover in a garage next door to our house, and they've pulled it into a million pieces. There's nothing left of it, only two rusty girders and four wheels!"

Then the man from Norfolk rang up when I'd returned to Bolton and said, "Really, you know – I've chewed a bit too much off. This chassis – it's had it, beyond repair!" He went on he'd put out on the internet to other Land Rover dealerships and what have you, part-mart makers, all of that for a new chassis. He succeeded in getting one; he got a brand-new heavy-duty galvanised chassis, made in Stockport by a man called Mr Marsland.

Then the rebuilding with the V8 engine commenced. In the end, when desperation had set in to get it back, it was still unfinished. I rang him one day to ask how it was going, and told him the director wanted it back for the filming.

Anyway, one weekend they brought it. I must say, it looked very splendid and nice and shiny. It looked like brand-new, but old fashioned. Just the job! But the thing is, this V8 engine is more like a formula-1 racing car. At the traffic lights, it takes off like buggery. Also, the petrol consumption's doubled!

The bloody sad thing is though, it didn't get back in time to be included in the new set of filming, so we had to use footage of the last stuff filmed for 'Industrial Age' instead. A great pity that, but no doubt it will be included in the next programmes if there are any...'

They've got your Land Rover in a garage next door to our house, and they've pulled it into a million pieces. There's nothing left of it, only two rusty girders and four wheels!

Fred on Fame
By Fred Dibnah

I reckon the only thing that's ever changed about me nowadays is the size of the bloody crowd when I'm telling me stories on a steam rally or in a pub! Fame has never altered me: I've always been the same since being a very young man. When you see them blokes on telly, with their fancy ways and funny clothes, I think, "What the hell have you ever done to be famous for?" I was never any good at telling jokes, and I didn't think it was all that important anyway. Me mam wanted me to play the piano, and me dad was a good dancer, like our kid. I wanted to be like the men up in the sky who were like gods to me when I was a small boy, and I was lucky enough to end up making my living from being like them, mending factory chimneys.

One of my earliest memories weren't about a factory chimney, but a domestic one! There were a neighbour in the next-but-one street called Mr Tranter, a bit posher than we were because their house had leaded windows, and they were always having their front door painted with them funny patterns done with a heart-grainer to resemble wood, like they used to do back then.

One day, I noticed a bit of a commotion outside their house, and I went over to see what the matter was. Mr Tranter told me their cat, Blackie, had got stuck up the parlour chimney or summat. I went in to see if I could do owt, but the bloody thing started hissing and spitting at me when I eventually shoved a brush steel up the chimney to try and dislodge the creature. (It's a bit like that time later on in me life when I were mending a factory chimney and a cat got stuck up there one day after going up the ladder, and I had to try and rescue it).

Anyway, this bloody cat of Mr Tranter's wouldn't come down, and then suddenly – whoosh! A great cloud of black soot all over Mrs Tranter's posh hearthrug, and I remember thinking, "I bet the poor bugger would be more terrified of his wife's reaction to that happening when she came back from the shops than the damned cat being wedged up the chimney!"

Anyway, after I'd been on telly, the BBC and ITV were there pointing their cameras skywards at me when I rescued the cat from the top of a factory chimney. The cat, a red one, (which, after it had been up the chimney all night, was a black one the following morning!), ended up being on all the local news items, and I got letters from cat lovers from all over the place. Funny thing this fame: I can tell you tales like that, but if you ask me where I was doing one of me after-dinner talks last week, I couldn't tell you. I'm not that bothered about being famous.

Hell, before the telly came along, I never ventured far away from home. I'd lie awake in my bed some nights thinking, "If I had a few grand in the bank, I could finish me engine, and not bother about money so much." But you've gotta get on in this life, and it's an ill wind that blows no bugger any good. So, to be honest, I don't mind it so much when people come from all over the country down to my yard to see me. I mean, it's all right because some of 'em bring me interesting stuff for me garden without me havin' to part with any green notes, so it's not that bad being famous!

Fred's Chimney
By Fred Dibnah

In the year 2000 a reporter from the local press went along to Radcliffe Road, Bolton, to ask Fred Dibnah about Fred's latest creation – a 45ft-high chimney stack that he had built in his back garden! Scratching his chin and posing for the photographer, Fred stood proudly gazing up at the brick-built structure and said, "I've knocked down a fair few chimneys in me life, but really, I've not built too many. The thing is, it's been eight years in the making. And I think it'll probably be the last-ever chimney stack built in Bolton. There's not many left now, but at one time, when I were a kid, they were all over the place. I built a rather fancy chimney on me mam's house when I were about 17, but when I started me steam workshops, after I were married, like, I always reckoned I'd build another on a grander scale when I got time. This bugger's been done in dribs and drabs over the years, you see. I've always been on with other stuff, but it's worth it now, because it'll have me steam boiler and all the tackle running more efficiently. The top looks like stone, but it's not, it's concrete, and I made a mould out of some of them modern blue-plastic 45-gallon oil drums cut down, and pieces of wood to give it the shape, then poured in the concrete and hoisted it up to the top with a block and tackle. I had a bit of a 'topping out' ceremony with the missus and that was filmed by the man from the BBC. Think he thought we were a bit barmy, because we had our wind-up horn gramophone up there too. Rather nice, though. They did a lot of that in the old days when the steeplejacks had finished building the thing."

Fred said, I think my garden chimney will be the last true brick chimney that will ever be built in Bolton.

WANT SOMETHING DIFFERENT FROM BOLTON?

Fred Dibnah was the world's formost steeplejack and steam enthusiast. So why not employ this much loved famous name to promote your product or event?

Sheila Dibnah has a growing reputation as an excellent guest speaker and word is travelling fast!

Using all her skills and perception based on a career spanning over 30 years in the entertainment industry, this other native of Bolton, Fred's glamorous widow Sheila delivers remarkably accurate and entertaining talk focusing on life and times with Fred Dibnah MBE and all he stood for. No one else can give you the real 'nuts and bolts' of the nation's favourite steeplejack and television presenter. Sheila can speak for anything from 30 minutes to an hour and half, and if required can participate in prior radio and media interviews at no extra charge, generating as much public interest as possible and ensuring your event is a complete success.

This is truly "The Other Half of Fred Dibnah" – don't miss this exciting opportunity to lift the cap on the worlds most celebrated steeplejack.

Hear the stories, laugh at his antics!

Be amazed at the candour and wicked impersonations!

Available for daytime or night time events throughout the country from small informal gatherings to corporate dinners or charity money raising events, Sheila aims at providing a versatile, fun packed professional and informative appearance to suit your needs.

Booking NOW for after dinner talks, steam rally appearance work, promotional marketing events, cruise line bookings, television and modelling work. Or any event or presentation where you need that bit of extra sparkle with a northern flavour!

See www.fredtalks.co.uk for further details or contact Nikki Walsh on 07948 333650.

No sole agent.

Member of NMTF

The Early Days
By Michael Webber

My Friend Fred

At the end of Fred's life he let it be known his work as a steeplejack had always held the greatest passion and fascination for him throughout the decades, despite his unchallenged expertise as a steam engineer and, later, television historian. With the nature of this type of work, a steeplejack of long ago must have been a rare breed of men, and many of them wrote colourful biographies about some of their experiences. The oldest one I have in my possession, written by James Wright was published in1886. Wright didn't know the year of his birth apparently, but his book "Steeplejacks Adventures" was completed after 45 years of climbing chimneys and steeples. A latter biography of 1926 by the very successful steeplejack William Larkins states...

"A really efficient Steeplejack must be a veritable Jack of all trades. He is to be a mason, a mechanic, a copper worker, scaffolder, carpenter & painter.

He must too learn slating, gold-leaf laying, soldering, sign writing and the principle of clocks."

I am sure we can all agree that Fred Dibnah was definitely an efficient Steeplejack. As a youngster I was drawn to this cheerful chappy, then unknown except locally as 'Fred'. He was always approachable and easily led into mischief. His first wife, Alison, was known on occasions to say to people "I don't know who's worst – Michael or Fred!"

Above everything else he was a magnificent teacher. We had many interests in common and in my most impressionable early teens he gave such systematic information to a willing student. I had complete respect for Fred and those around him such as Donald, his helper. There were never any raised words, unlike other teachers I'd had before. A lot of

Fred's appeal was the ever present danger of what he did. One of my first lessons in climbing a chimney was not to hold on to the ladder rungs. "What yer goin' to do, lad, if the rung yer've got hold of comes out in your hand?" he quipped on one occasion.

I always found that to get the best out of Fred you had to work as a team. He did his part, I did mine and I learnt from him, gaining much confidence in the process. And so began a unique and wonderful friendship with Fred Dibnah and his family. When I moved south, I didn't lose touch with the Dibnahs, and would visit their home as much as possible. I eventually became friendly with Fred's second family after his divorce from Alison, and later his widow Sheila and I became firm friends, a lady for whom I have the greatest respect and admiration.

Steam Up!

By the winter of 1972-3 the gear teeth in the roller were badly worn and had to be replaced. In Fred's words "they were diabolical and the noise they made were bloody horrendous". As usual when the roller was in bits, Fred made sure all those awkward, little engine parts that couldn't be accessed when the roller was complete were serviced, cleaned and painted. Everything was shiny and bright, but more importantly it was mechanical perfection: that became Fred's hallmark right up to the end of his days.

The great day dawned for a trial run, my instruction from Fred being, "Right, cock, make sure you are here at 10 o'clock." But when I got to Fred's house neither he nor the roller were to be seen! I followed the tracks left on the tarmac; they ended right outside the local public house, The Lever Bridge! This pub is situated at the bottom of an extremely steep hill, and to one side was some waste land. Fred always parked the roller in the same spot when visiting this pub, on the edge of the waste land nearest the car park, facing uphill.

Although under age to go into the premises, I was greeted by a cheerful Fred ready with my first-ever pint of Tetley's Mild. It turned out that the new gears exceeded Fred's expectations." There's none of that awful banging and bloody grinding! You can actually here the engine chuffing up the chimney! And there's no vibration!" he said, "The only problem now is we've run out of coal and we've got to get up that bloody mountain to get home!"

Fred's merry-making continued, and he imbibed a few more jars for good measure. Bored, I started looking around for a few sticks to keep the fire going. Around the waste land I found lots of wood – old garage doors, 3x2s, roof beams, all sorts of stuff. I knew most of them were too long to fit in the firebox but I made a little pile of various sizes next to the roller.

When Fred saw the wood he encouraged me to go back and get some more, saying he could break it up later. Well, it was going dark by then and Fred was getting hungry. The roller was blowing off hard now and a loud roaring noise was arousing much attention from passers-by and folk within the pub.

Fred announced, "I'm now going to light me lamps." To raucous shouts from members of the crowd, such as "You've got a flat tyre, mate!" or "You'll never get up that big hill with that thing!" Fred made his way to the front of the roller, but then had to confess that he couldn't light the lamps because he had forgotten to fill them with paraffin!

So Fred was nearly ready for off: "Plenty of steam and a belly full of water", he shouted to the crowd. All that was left to do was to break up some wood for the return journey. No problem: the wood was laid out on the pavement before the roller, with about two feet sticking into the road. 'Oh I see!' I thought to myself – 'he is going to roll over it and break it THAT way, this will certainly be fun to see'! I recall that Fred started jumping around like mad as he unexpectedly stood on a nail sticking out of a floor board and

accidentally caught a woman's dress standing in the crowd with a bit of the 3x2 plank! By then, as Fred began climbing up on to the footplate it was getting very late and the night was pitch black.

Slowly, Fred proceeded to roll over the wood which popped, banged, creaked and groaned under the 12-ton Aveling and Porter steam roller. At first the onlookers all stepped back in horror, but as they sensed there was no real danger, enthusiasm took over and they stepped forward even closer to witness the spectacle. "Come on, Fred, a bit more, Fred, a bit, more" they were all shouting.

With the rear roller three inches away from the high kerbstone the end result was a neatly-cut collection of firewood the correct length to fit in the firebox. Obviously, Fred knew exactly what he was doing. The wood was quickly loaded up into the tender; the rest was put on the fire in readiness for that return journey up the hill. This was one of my first outings with Fred on the roller where he wanted me to steer for him. I had never been down to the Lever Bridge pub before and I certainly wasn't prepared for what was to happen next.

about 120 r.p.m. and the exhaust beat gets louder & louder as the hill gets steeper: Chuff! Chuff! Chuff! Chuff!

Fred was in his element as sparks started to fly from the chimney top. Roaring with laughter as he sways around the footplate with his arms in the air, oil can in one hand, it's as if he is conducting a symphony orchestra. Fred nudged me to look behind at all the sparks and the crowd still watching the spectacle. The vacuum created by the massive load on the engine created in the smoke box sucked millions & millions of sparks and hot ashes from the fire bars and ash pan, and blasted them into the sky! At the steepest part of the hill the crankshaft slowed to about 100 r.p.m. That is 200 wonderful but ear-bashing chuffs a minute! One could sense the engine under this massive load as the torque increased and the noise emanating from the gearing changed to a deep hum, and the boiler pressure started to rise rapidly. By now the emissions from the chimney were 100% sparks with what looked like an orange searchlight shining skywards from the chimney top. The sparks shot 50 perhaps 60 feet into the air and spread to a huge

The roller had been burning wood for many hours now and with the crowd cheering and much whistle-blowing, we were heading up the veritable mountain in top gear! Just as in a car this would make the engine work very hard and you would have to 'put your foot down'. On the roller this action is the regulator which would now be referred to as being 'open'. On the footplate, the crankshaft is turning at

canopy before returning to the ground. At the brow of the hill the sparks gradually ceased and the crankshaft revs increased to a steady pace.

Drama at The Last Drop

Fred has told the story of the day that the front forks got smashed in a disaster at The Last Drop Village Hotel in Bolton on Sunday, October 20th 1974 so many times that I will not repeat it but simply add a few details.

The crash was the result of the roller getting out of control on a steep hill and hitting a concrete post. Fred immediately climbed up on to the footplate to shovel out the fire, which I had replenished just minutes before the incident. The roller came to rest at such a steep angle that most of the firebox crown was not covered in water. It was imperative that Fred removed the fire as soon as possible to prevent a major boiler explosion. He opened the fire hole door, and was engulfed in flames and smoke from the coal I had shovelled on previously. Next, he frantically tried to shovel out the fire, but he only had a stoking shovel which was far too short as all the fire was deep inside the boiler.

I was told to get some rags and drench them in cold water from the engine water tank. Fred wrapped these around his hands and fingers, which were by now badly burnt and blistered. After a frantic struggle, Fred was confident everything was safe and he came round to the front end. He turned to me and slowly stated, "Michael. Once I owned a steam roller, but look at this ruddy lot now, eh!" With that he threw the shovel to the ground and walked away.

Fortunately for Fred, it turned out that a gentleman by the name of Jack Hampshire of Dewsbury, Yorkshire had a spare front fork casting leaning on a wall in a shed, so Fred made arrangements to collect the spare casting from him.

Having a few days off work after the incident, Fred returned to the scene and set about fitting the new forks.

Prominently cast in bold letters on the new front forks are the details '10 TON'. This specifies the class of roller they are designed to fit. The forks that got smashed were '12 TON'. So at least Fred took some consolation knowing that now his roller had the correct size front forks! They were a slightly different shape, which Fred preferred and he was intrigued to imagine how his roller ended up with the wrong size forks.

The following Saturday I went with Fred to bring the engine home. On arrival the roller looked sorry for itself and was unusually dirty, something never seen before. The copper pipe and non-return valve to the injector was bent and twisted. I could see that the bottom of the smoke box was all bent and badly dented, meaning the door didn't close properly. Although the replacement forks were rough and extremely rusty, Fred fettled the engine like new, and before long, he was his old self again, for now he had lots of new stories he could tell!

When we got to the top of the big hill on the way back I remember clutching on to the steering wheel very hard, mostly out of fear! It was not very often that I saw Fred worried, but to make sure the roller didn't get out of control this time, he decided to go

down the hill backwards. 'Oh great – so I have got to steer the thing backwards for half a mile!' I thought to myself.

Fred made sure that the brakes were screwed on very tightly and we set off from the top of the hill going backwards in the slow gear.

The next day, undeterred, Fred made sure the engine would not be out of action for long. Saturday evening saw him taking off the bent non-return valve, annealing and straightening it back as it should be. By the time I arrived on Sunday, the fire in the engine was lit and Fred was just reshaping the copper pipe from the injector that connected to the non-return valve.

So off we headed with the engine, towards the Lever Bridge pub. Approaching the pub, Fred spotted a road which was very narrow and cobbled. He said "Turn up here, Michael. We're goin' ter go on a detour now, cock". After a short distance we turned left into what looked like a field. It was just grass, bare earth and had large lumps of rock sticking up out of the ground – the waste land that I mentioned earlier, where I'd collected the wood! The land sloped very

steeply downhill, and in the distance I could see the River Tong in full flow.

Just as I feared, as soon as the rear rollers came upon the big rocks, the engine went out of control again. My stomach churned as I pretended this was great fun and glanced up to see Fred grinning like a Cheshire cat. I just closed my eyes at that point, as any steering on my part made no difference, and we were just going sideways! So this was off-roading on a steam roller, eh! When we gradually came to a halt Fred assured me there was no way we would end up in the river and just carried on regardless, messing at the controls of the engine. He seemed full of confidence, and I was amazed at his bravery as he got us out of difficulties.

After about half an hour we ended up in the usual spot just next to the Lever Bridge public house car park!

A Trip with a Happy Ending

On a beautiful midsummer day, Fred and I were in the roller, returning to Bolton from an event at the East Lancs Railway Museum at Bury. Passing the newly-repaired Bury Parish Church, we glanced up at the repaired weathervane, where Fred's gold-leaf gleamed in the sunshine. I had recently been on top of the spire with Fred and it was still fresh in our minds. A large part of the work had been pointing around the top and Eddie Chatwood, a fellow steeplejack and good mate, had come along to

experience working with Fred's mastic. Fred knew that the master steeplejack, John Faulkner of Salford had devised a mastic very different from what you could buy, so Fred had been experimenting with mastic of various compositions and had formulated one with the capabilities that he required. Fred never used sand and cement for this type of work, considering it useless since it sets too hard and does not then have the necessary amount of 'give' in it to allow tall factory chimneys and church spires to bend and sway in strong winds, as they must do.

After we had travelled a few miles down the A58, Fred spied his first pub, and the establishment had a fire hydrant conveniently located nearby, so we stopped. All refreshed, full of water and oiled up, we set off again at our standard speed of one pub an hour! Fred was in control of the fire, regulator and the water level in the boiler, my job was steering this Rolls Royce of steam rollers with its new gears. It was wonderful to be able to talk to each other rather than having to shout at the top of your voice!

We were probably halfway home by now and the leisurely pace gave us opportunity to look at the scenery and relax a little. We could see for miles right over Little Lever, Radcliffe, Salford and Manchester and beyond.

Just a little further along the road Fred stopped the engine and pulled into the kerb just opposite some imposing Edwardian terraced houses standing high above the road, enjoying the spectacular views towards Manchester. Leaving me to tend the fire and fill the boiler, Fred went to call on someone who lived there. He returned a few minutes later with a man called Howarth. I think this was Frank Howarth, the works foreman or manager to one of Bolton's oldest engineering works Hick Hargreaves, the firm established by Benjamin Hick in 1832.

History books say that the first public railway was the Liverpool and Manchester that was built in 1830. In actual fact, the world's first public railway ran from Bolton to Leigh and was opened in 1828. The Bolton

railways. The stone is lighter in colour, and quite different from the main body of the church. Naturally it was one of Fred's many ambitions to ladder this wonderful creation. He was recorded doing so in a programme from the 'Magnificent Monuments' series by David Hall. At over 300 feet high this was to be the last spire or tall structure Fred climbed using his own ladders and equipment.

Anyway, just across the road from Hicks entrance is a pub called 'The Sweet Green Tavern'. When the old hard seat benches that had rested against the wall for nearly 150 years were ripped out, amongst the detritus behind them were some hand-drawn, but nevertheless accurate, engineer's drawings. They were carefully gathered up and taken to the nearby museum. Eventually the news came back that they had been accredited to be the work of George Stephenson's son, Robert Stephenson, and Ben Hick. The Hicks works built early locomotives in Bolton, some being to Brunel's design. Fred spoke in awe of these important pioneering engineers sitting drawing, and exchanging ideas in the little pub just a few yards from where Hicks works now stood. Fred was then eager to show Mr. Howarth the recent work carried out, in particular the new gears which I assume were manufactured at Hicks.

and Leigh train was hauled by a little locomotive named 'The Lancashire Witch'. Interestingly, when Alison had deserted Fred to his own devices in 1985, Fred seriously considered that 'The Lancashire Witch' should be the new name for his roller!

When the wooden sleeper system was perfected, all the stone blocks upon which the rails were previously secured became redundant. The spire of St. Walburgs Church in Preston is the 2nd or 3rd highest in England and is entirely built of those old stone blocks from the Bolton and Leigh, and Liverpool and Manchester

They wanted to park the roller in the back street behind the house. The back street was even higher up the bank than the house! First, we had to get the roller up an unmade road to reach the street, over great lumps of rocks, gullies and high protruding manhole covers. The back street was cobbled with those great big things like loaves of bread! The roller was duly reversed down the back street, making one hell of a din in the process.

Leaving me to try to placate neighbours angry at this thing disturbing their nice afternoon, Fred and Mr Howarth went back to the house. Mr Howarth reappeared some time later with a plate of cheese butties and told me that he had first met Fred when he was employed to patch up some of the slated roofs of the Hicks buildings. Fred was desperate for help with his back axle and bearings for the roller and asked if Mr. Howarth would take a look if it was transported there on the back of his Land Rover. He, Mr Howarth, agreed and the axle was set up on stands in a quiet corner of the works. On examination, the axle was found to have worn down by about a sixteenth of an inch towards the ends, where the bearings were located. Basically, it needed

a bit shaving off the middle section, about twenty inches in length. Fred earned great respect throughout the works by doing the job by hand-filing the axle to a useable condition to within a tolerance of five thousand parts of an inch.

Time was marching on and Fred had to consider the couple of hour's journey to get home. A hose pipe took care of the water for the roller and Mr Howarth decided it would be a grand opportunity to get rid of his coal bunker if Fred would take the coal. (Bolton had become a 'smokeless zone'). Fred reluctantly agreed and we all got covered in massive cobwebs, bugs and coal in removing it to the roller. Mr Howarth generously presented Fred and me with clean white shirts from his wardrobe! Fred's was a reasonable fit but mine with an 18 inch collar and 50 inch chest kept everyone laughing for some time.

A little attention to oiling of parts, a shovelling of a great heap of the old coal on to the fire and were ready to return to what Fred often referred to as "the Queens Highway." The old coal produced about 400% more smoke than usual, much to the disgust of the neighbours as they were engulfed in smoke that

temporarily eclipsed the summer sun! "So much for the smokeless zone!" was Fred's comment!

Nearing the outskirts of Bolton, everything was running very well. I had an inkling Fred had been drinking with Mr. Howarth by the very fast speed of the crankshaft when we reached a point where the road had a long straight bit ahead with a bus stop at the kerb. The perfect place for him shovelling on more coal and keeping an eye on the road without having to touch the regulator.

The area of the bus stop was made of concrete, on which I had had no driving experience. Fred was tending the fire when suddenly, as we hit the patch, there was a huge earthquake. Everything started vibrating and shaking violently. The oil cans went up in the air. Shaken and very worried I turned to see what Fred was doing just in time to catch him doing a spectacular backward somersault, landing flat on his back in the middle of the road still holding the coal shovel! I was really quite impressed! Another of many memorable occasions!

After stopping the roller as quickly as possible I couldn't help bursting out in uncontrollable laughter. Fortunately, there had been a lull in the traffic and so he didn't get run over. As quick as a flash he was back on his feet, and we laughed and laughed until it was painful!

From here it was an uneventful but interesting journey, down hill, up hill until we finally, arrived back at Fred's house, known locally as 'Two Cats'. The name deriving from the two cats or lions of the Earl of Bradford's coat of arms as prominently displayed at the front of the house.

Royal Air Force, Burtonwood

By Fred Dibnah

A historic landmark at RAF Burtonwood near Liverpool was brought to a crashing end in April 1988. Originally 'Number 37 Maintenance Unit', RAF Burtonwood provided Spitfires to the beleaguered 'Few' during 'The Battle of Britain' in 1940 before being taken over by the United States Army Air Corps. It became the 'Base Air Depot' for the 8th US Air Force then additionally the 9th and ultimately the 12th and 15th Air Forces as well, becoming probably the largest military base in Europe during World War II, providing over 11,500 aircraft between 1943 and 1945.

So steeplejacks Fred Dibnah and Eddy Chattwood arrived at Burtonwood in April 1988, under contract to 'Atherton Demolition' to demolish the control tower. It stood on six reinforced-concrete legs, each being 18 inches square. Three legs were carefully removed using six-inch steel-mesh rock drills and a gas-axe, (oxy-acetylene burner, to burn away the metal reinforcements), each leg being replaced by four cut-down telegraph poles. Eddy Chattwood, who worked with Fred from 1968 onwards and assisted on many of Fred's early demolition jobs, says that he and Fred had to work in very windy conditions on the day of the drop and so three big fires had to be lit to burn away the temporary supports. "Fred and I and were both spooked that day by the constant banging of corrugated-metal sheets and the howling wind. It was like we weren't meant to be there and was very scary", he said. But within 23 minutes the structure collapsed, and as it did so the final aerial armada left RAF Burtonwood from a window halfway up the control tower – a family of ducks! Atherton Demolition invited everyone to a hospitality marquee after the drop. "It was decorated like a wedding reception", commented Eddy, "All that was missing was the bride and groom. Still, it was a free bar!"

Fred and I and were both spooked that day by the constant banging ....

Burtonwood broke many records during and after WWII with it being the biggest, best, fastest and most efficient of all bases. Nicknamed 'Lancashire's Detroit' and visited by everyone from The Duke of Edinburgh, General Montgomery,
General Eisenhower, General Patton, Bob Hope, Bing Crosby and James Cagney, this base was unique.

Cockermouth Mill Chimney Drop, Cockermouth, Cumbria.
By Alan McEwen

It was Saturday, 8th November, 1992. It was unusual for Fred to drop a chimney on a Saturday, but the coming Sunday was special: Remembrance Sunday, and Fred being a very superstitious chap, Remembrance Sunday was out. Fred, Neil Carney and Eddy Chattwood, the Ramsbottom steeplejack, had worked for most of the preceding week on the preparation for the drop. The tall, octagonal and extremely graceful mill chimney had a massive, square, stone pedestal and a tapering barrel constructed from brick. I and my family motored up the A65 and M6 to Cockermouth on receiving Fred's usual cordial invite to the chimney drop. On arrival on the site, I noticed that in a large area of the mill yard, for quite a considerable distance over to the left of the mill chimney's location, a large crowd of 'punters' were gathering. There was a small admittance charge of about 50 pence each, the cash being destined to go to a charity. To the front of the crowd was a silver band from Carlisle.

On reaching the foot of the chimney I quickly realised that the 'gobbed out' front and sides of the pedestal had suffered a serious fire: the pink sandstone masonry being blackened with a large lump lying close to the front of the chimney base. Whilst I was engaged in firing off a few photographs, Fred suddenly appeared, but didn't look his usual radiant, friendly self. He looked tired, almost haggard. He greeted me with, "Hiya Al. Look what some bloody-minded sods have done. Some buggers in the wee small hours of this morning have bloody crept into the mill yard and lit the demolition bonfire!" The bonfire had been stacked under the chimney in readiness for the big event that afternoon.

Fred went on to relate how he and his two mates, Neil and Eddy, had been awakened early that morning at their lodgings by the police and fire brigade. They requested that Fred attend the mill site most urgently, as vandals had lit the bonfire, resulting in all of the telegraph-pole props being burnt away and the 180-feet chimney being left apparently rocking to and fro in the light breeze. Fred was urged by the emergency service chiefs to make safe this deadly, towering stack post haste. Fred and Eddy Chattwood, (as related to me by Fred himself), were pretty much still full of best bitter after spending the

previous evening in a local hostelry, and were therefore, apparently not very tuned in for the exceedingly deadly work expected of them by the local fire brigade. Neil, however, was a dedicated teetotaller, and although physically very tired was feeling quite alert. Shortly following the chimney-toppling trio's arrival at the base of the unstable chimney, the dangerous work of clearing away the messy detritus of the partially-burnt bonfire materials quickly got underway, followed by the fixing of new timber support props,. Fred recalled later that despite the cold and drizzly weather, he had been thoroughly soaked through with sweat dripping from every pore due to the anxiety and stress he and his two chums had to endure. Eventually with the new props in place and the chimney safe, they could all sigh with relief and Fred, Eddy and Neil became the heroes of the Cumbrian police and fire service.

I left Fred to go about his work and climbed on to the flat-topped mill roof via several flights of internal stone stairs with the aim of setting up my camera tripods in a location which overlooked the mill chimney. On looking over the parapet I could easily see Fred at the base of the stack clearing away some compressed air pipelines in readiness for the lighting of the bonfire at 3 pm.

Because Fred had kindly invited my ten-year-old son, Alasdair, to actually light the bonfire materials which had been stacked into the 'gobbed out' void at the base of the pedestal, I then hurried down the hundreds of stone steps clutching a camera which would enable me to record the event on film.

At 3 o'clock precisely, Alasdair, with Fred's direction, lit the bonfire. Glancing over to the burgeoning crowd of Cumbrian folk who could view the proceedings at a safe distance, I could also see and then hear the band break into tune. Within a few minutes the fire had taken hold and was burning furiously. Ensuring that Alasdair was safe with my family and friends, I then scurried back up the stone steps and on to the mill roof to take my photographs. I could hear the tall chimney roaring melodramatically with its tubular-shaped innards sucking in voluminous amounts of orangey-hued flame. Black smoke poured in great gouts from the chimney's cap. The birds'-eye view from my position was a profoundly colourful one, with the small Cumbrian town lying beyond the beautiful, silvery River Derwent and with the Lakeland hills on the skyline.

Fred's expert calculations for the drop allowed for the stack to fall and land on the concrete mill yard parallel to the river and approximately a couple of hundred feet from the bank. However, due to the fire damage caused to the pedestal by the vandals, fate would play its hand, and all would not go precisely to plan.

On the roof and firing off shots, I was suddenly joined by two well-dressed gentlemen togged up in tweeds who introduced themselves as directors of the mill company. Both were very interested and well excited. The fire had been raging now for about twenty-five minutes. The tallest of the tweed-clad gentlemen very politely asked me how long the chimney would remain standing. "Any minute now it should start to fall," I replied. I had already informed them both that I was a close friend of Fred and had attended numerous chimney-demolition jobs.

Another ten minutes ticked by with the chimney still upright. Looking over the parapet I could make out that the bonfire had burned itself out and very little smoke was now issuing from the chimney top. The tall tweedy chap could obviously guess that something was amiss. "Has the fire gone out?" he asked, "And if the chimney doesn't fall this afternoon", (the late-autumn afternoon which had been sunny was now turning into evening and getting darker by the minute), "Will Mr. Dibnah return and knock it down tomorrow?" the man asked. Well, I obviously put him right by informing him that within the next few minutes the chimney would indeed topple. I looked over the parapet again and in the gloom below could make out the small flat-capped figure of Fred carrying a jack-hammer whilst pulling on the trailing airlines behind. Fred moved from the rear of the fire-ravaged chimney to breakout some more of the stonework on the 'blind side' of the pedestal. This was the opposite side to where the large lump of stone had previously fallen off following the act of vandalism. I then heard Fred hammering away, the cacophony rising and filling my ears.

What a dreadfully-dangerous position for Fred to be in! (I later learned that Eddy was at his side with Neil quite close, too – both steeplejacks extremely brave men). The tweedy man questioned me again. "He won't leave the chimney will he? Is there something wrong?" "No way, Fred will bring it down," I said somewhat exasperated. Then – movement in the tall, tapering stack! "It's going!" I said, whilst I fired off a sequence of shots with my Olympus OM 1.

The chimney toppled gracefully and crashed down to land just slightly over to the right of the projected fall-line, and a massive cloud of dust rose I heard a female voice half-scream, half-shout "FRED!". I looked over again. Fred was nowhere to be seen. I was mortified with thoughts of my close friend Fred being buried and pulped under countless tons of brick and stone. Still looking down, transfixed, the dust and murk slightly easing, I espied a solitary figure complete with oily flat cap emerge from behind the shattered remains of the chimney's pedestal. I then heard the distinctive Boltonian accent and the triumphant, well-known cry - "Did yer like that?" Fred was safe, although covered from head to toe in dust.

After the drop, as pre-arranged, Fred and his family, together with ourselves and close friends such as Neil and Francis Carney and Eddy Chattwood drove the 80- odd miles down to our home at Farling Top, where we all enjoyed a grand old bash in the farmhouse after letting off fireworks at a huge bonfire I had built in the bottom fields.

Whilst sitting around the bonfire enjoying a couple of bottles of Guinness, Fred blamed the bad luck regarding the chimney drop on a 'weird man' who had visited the pub in Cockermouth where Fred had been propping up the bar. Apparently, this individual was a salesman for a local firm of undertakers who had presented Fred with a pencil which had the name of the undertaking firm emblazoned in gold print on it. Fred seriously blamed the problems experienced with the chimney on this rather innocent gesture. He was an extremely superstitious character, was Fred. God bless him.

The Farnworth Chimney Drop

Fred Dibnah, demolition expert and television celebrity, had mixed feelings of job satisfaction yet regret when he felled the last 19th century, red-brick chimney still standing in Farnworth near Bolton, Lancashire. The site of the BPC works had suffered fire damage and it was decided on safety grounds that the chimney should be demolished. As well as clearing the way for site improvements, the demolition meant that residents in nearby Mather Street would not have to be disturbed by traffic, (a new road was to be built through the ground where the chimney was standing).

Fred said, "This is a beautiful example of a chimney, lovely red-brick and in good condition. It's a shame you can't just lift them up and put them somewhere else. I know lots of places that would love a chimney like this."

The Chairman of BPC, Mike Wilson, said, "Fred got it exactly right, the chimney fell down where it was supposed to. But I must admit I did have my fingers crossed at the time." Locals and television crews gathered to see the stack fall and, according to Fred, "The job went smoothly – not a hitch!"

FRED DIBNAH LTD

121 RADCLIFFE ROAD, BOLTON BL2 1NU. TEL & FAX 01204 531903

Fully insured repairs of
Chimneys and Church Spires.
Flag Poles painted. Chimneys felled and demolished or
banded and pointed. Weather Vanes and
Lightning Conductors made to order and fitted.
Industrial Archaeological Restoration projects undertaken.

CHIMNEY REPAIRER

STEEPLEJACK

ESTABLISHED 1958

17th October 1991

To the Occupier,

We would like to inform you that at 3pm on Friday 18th October 1991
the chimney at Cone Works, Mather Street, Farnworth is to be demolished.

As your premises are in close proximity to the site we are informing you
that you must vacate your home for the duration of the operation.
This will be for approximately ½ hour 3pm – 3.30pm.

We apologise for any inconvenience that this may cause.

Yours faithfully

Fred Dibnah.

Registered Number 3504921 England and Wales

V.A.T. No. 719 729 888

Fred Dibnah Visits "The Great Dorset Steam Fair"
By Paul Donoghue

It was after Fred had dropped a lovely red-brick chimney at Farnworth that I asked him if he would like to visit The Great Dorset Steam Fair. The yearly event is held on 600 acres of farmland near a village called Tarrant Hinton near Blandford, Dorset, and is reputed to be the biggest steam event in the world, attracting almost 250,000 visitors and exhibitors. Fred said, "I don't know if I can go, cock; you see, her who must be obeyed has the diary, and Dorset's bloody miles away". I told Fred that I would pay all his expenses, including a caravan on the site. Looking back, how could our hero possibly refuse? I didn't get an answer straight away, it was obvious that Fred was working on the wife and playing the 'softly, softly, catchee monkey' game.

Several weeks went by and The Great Dorset Steam Fair date was getting closer. Fred was having a 'steam day' at Glynllifon Parc in Wales, (where he had totally restored a beam engine), and I was driving him there. I told Fred that I had spoken to Michael Oliver, (organiser of the Fair), who had said that, if Fred came, he would lay on a top-class caravan for him in

the best area on the site, near the entrance to the beer tents and the Fair. Fred sat bolt upright and said, "Didn't I tell you, cock? We're going, that's been decided over a month. Bloody hell, cock, me brains turning to mash, thought I'd told you? I just hope it doesn't rain like last time I went there, it was like six inches of Aero chocolate, and it was that bad you couldn't get to the beer tent. My roller never moved, in fact nothing really moved; it was what they call one of those disasters". I was amazed that Fred hadn't told me he was coming to Dorset, but you can imagine my delight that he was!

..... I don't know if I can go, cock; you see, her who must be obeyed has the diary ....

I made the long drive to The Great Dorset Steam Fair a couple of days before it was due to start, wanting to make sure that everything had been properly arranged by Michael Oliver. I had learnt the previous year that Michael has his own way of running events, with a complaints procedure that is second to none. If someone were to have a complaint, Michael would invariably say, "I'm just sorting this feller out over here and I'll be with you in 10 minutes", and promptly jump in his car and drive half a mile to the other side of the site and have breakfast! His philosophy was, he once told me, "I ain't got no time to sort out 300 problems at once and people have a funny way of sorting things out by themselves. Everyone here is a showman of some description, and who can blame them for wanting to be at the front or pinching a bit of someone's plot? When I go home from here, my head hits the pillow and I'm straight to sleep. If I was to take on 300 problems at once, I'd be in the bloody river by March!"

Later that day, I did have a complaint of my own – the top-class caravan turned out to be a two-wheeled, 3-berth wreck that looked like it had been saved from a November the 5th bonfire party! Could I really allow the great Fred Dibnah to reside in such a vehicle?

I marched over to Michael Oliver, "Bloody hell, Michael, I thought you said top class! It's an absolute bloody wreck and a disgrace", I stormed. Michael gave me a sheepish look and said, "I'm sorry Paul – someone must have bloody cocked it up. I'll find out who's responsible and be back to you in 10 minutes. Rest assured this will be sorted out, I told them it was for Fred Dibnah!" Michael then disappeared, a little more quickly than usual! Do I need to finish this story?

Absolutely incensed, I spent the rest of the day scrubbing that caravan, buying pillows, air fresheners, towels, carpets, pots, pans etc. Only after a few hours did it dawn on me that he'd done one of his 'half-mile specials! Michael was right! By that time I had turned a wreck of a caravan into something that looked 100 per cent better than when I had first seen it. One up to Michael Oliver!

Fred arrived at the event a couple of days later with wife No2. I showed them to their caravan, fully expecting World War III to break out! Fred just stepped into the caravan, scratched his chin and made himself comfortable. I came back 10 minutes later and over a brew he asked me about the running order for filming, and what time did I need him in the morning? He never once mentioned that the caravan was a wreck. I can only assume that on the way to Wales, I had spoken into his deaf ear!

Fred was up bright and early on the first morning of filming and was having a wash and a shave on a table outside the caravan when I got there. It has always amazed me that when Fred has his cap off nobody recognised him. Steam and Fred Dibnah fans would walk past him and not have a clue as to who he was! But stick his cap and glasses on, and a crowd would develop in minutes.

Fred's first encounter of the morning was with (the late) Jack Wharton. Jack was one of the founding members of the National Traction Trust; he was a former president who was held in very high regard by every steam man: when Jack spoke, people listened. He was also an accomplished engineer and knew the workings of steam and traction engines inside out. Jack was a marvellous character who I had filmed and interviewed many times. Fred and Jack were chuckling about Dr Giles Romanies having to attend to a patient in the middle of the night while dressed like Rip Van Winkle in his nightshirt!

..... *It was at this stage that I realized that I could have made a huge mistake and a catastrophic error in judgment* ....

Our next stop was (the late) Chris Edmond's 'Pilgrim Steam Railway'. Fred and Chris got on like a house on fire, talking about the old days and the history of the miniature steam railway. Fred loved the little railway and couldn't wait to take the controls himself. As I remember it, Fred drove the engine for over half an hour, much to the delight of the fast-growing queue of passengers. It was at this stage that I realized that I could have made a huge mistake in having brought Fred to one of the biggest events in the country where thousands of members of the

public wanted to be near him. You could hear it again and again, "FRED DIBNAH IS OVER THERE!" As we tried to make our film, people totally ignored us but they would jostle to get near Fred. "Can you just sign this program, Fred, make it to aunt Daisy". "Can we have a photo, Fred?" "Fred, will you say "Did yer like that?" for my dad, he's always wanted to hear it live". Then the press came, "Over here, Fred", "Smile, Fred", "Look that way, Fred." "Look this way, Fred." As the day wore on you could see that Fred was getting fed up. "Bloody hell, Paul" he said, "I've never signed so many autographs in my life, I've got writer's cramp".

We discussed the situation that evening and decided that we would start earlier, 8am, and finish at 1pm. Between 11am and 1pm we would have Fred signing autographs at our trade stand, after which he would be free to do what he liked.

I caught up with Fred having a pint in one of the smaller beer tents late one afternoon. He'd taken off his cap and was enjoying some peace and quiet. An old chap who had three cameras round his neck plus a variety of lenses walked up to me and said in a posh voice, "I've been told that Fred Dibnah is somewhere round here. Could you possibly direct me to him?" Fred lifted his finger to his lips, so I said, "You've just missed him, sir, he's gone to the other side of the site looking for Michael Oliver." After the man had scurried off, Fred and I had a two-hour session sampling the delights of a master brewer, laughing and enjoying each other's company. For the first time since Fred had arrived at the Fair he was very relaxed and at peace with himself. The stories he told, the knowledge he passed to me, plus the pure delight of being with a genius made all my worries about a filming disaster go away.

I didn't collect enough footage to make a one-hour programme, the end result was only a small film of Fred at The Great Dorset Steam Fair, which we included in our master production, simply called – The Great Dorset Steam Fair.

The Worlds Largest Steam Rally

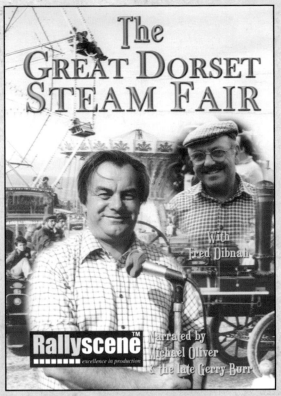

The Great Dorset Steam Fair.
See More Fred Dibnah on this DVD

More Fred Dibnah on this DVD.
Only - £8.50
**Plus £1.50 U.K.
Postage & Packing**

This unique video covers the history of the world's largest steam fair. From its humble beginnings to the massive event that it is today.

During the making of this DVD Rallyscene have called upon a huge resource of material. There are many unseen photographs, rare cine films and great interviews with people who have been with The Great Dorset Steam Fair since the early days. The main commentary is taken up by Michael Oliver along with comments and views from the late Gerry Burr.

Comments from the late Fred Dibnah, John Wharton, and the late Jack Wharton, Richard Preston, Chris Edmonds, Jim Sarney, and Roger Burville.

The DVD contains special features:
Prestons of Potto - Jim Sarney's 'The Story of Sad Sam'

RUNNING TIME 90 minutes

NOW HALF PRICE

www.freddibnah.tv   Order your goods. On-line 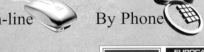   By Phone    or by Post

RALLYSCENE
The Pond House,
59 Rotherham Road,
Clowne, Derbyshire,
S43 4PT

Rallyscene ™
excellence in production

If you live outside the U.K. please phone to find out the postage rates for your country

The Great Canvey Island Chimney Disaster
by Fred and Sheila Dibnah

This is a story about knocking down a 450-foot-high concrete chimney, 11 inches thick, weighing about 2,500 tons. In my opinion, it was bordering on failure before I even touched it!

Having never been to Canvey in my life, we set off towards Essex. As we got close I could see in the distance a lot of concrete pipes, silver pipes, cream steam, black steam, all sorts of stuff, and amongst it there's a very large chimney sticking up. I'm thinking to myself, 'I hope to God it's not that!'

We steam on to site and are met by Rodney and his mate (from Health and Safety); these guy's looked like they had come straight from university, brand new rigger boots and shiny tin hats. Rodney says, "How many tons will one of your pit props hold up?"

Well, I've got this little book, "Aneurin Bevin – Timber in Mining, 1942", thick wartime edition, and it's got details of how to make the pit props for the mining men. Apparently a piece of wood five inches diameter and four feet long will hold 50-odd tons. I told this to Rodney and his mate; they looked at me with disbelief.

The main contractor, a gentleman called Mr Skudder from London, was there and he wanted to blow the arse out of it with dynamite and have all the glory. They had built this great bandstand with a corrugated iron roof, staircases, handrails, kicking boards, fully seated and everything for the 'civic dignitaries' of Canvey Island so they could sit and watch the drop.

......we're going to use the bottom bits, the bits that dogs pee on, where they're a lot thicker. I replied.

When the telegraph poles arrived, somebody had been buggering about with them – there were a four-foot length missing out of one end. I'm suspicious of this, so when Rodney and his mate arrived I said, "What have you been doing with my telegraph poles?" Rodney says, "We did a test, it held 58 tons before it busted". "Well, we're going to use the bottom bits, the bits that dogs pee on, where they're a lot thicker". I replied.

We set to work and are averaging about five feet a day with the Stihl saw 2½ inches in, and a CP9 jigger pick, which is the smallest demolition pick you can get. Now the secret weapon was Big Bertha. You've seen Irishmen in the road with a big drill? Well it's like one of them, but adapted to work sideways.

Every day Rodney and his mate would come and have a look. "Well there's no real weight on the wood yet is there, Rodney?" and off they would go; these lads were really earning their brass.

Over the next few days we're doing well. We're about five feet off halfway on the left-hand side. It doesn't do to go to the pub for your lunch too early when you're doing work of this nature, but I'd said to my wife, Sheila, "We'll see you at the pub at 1 o'clock."

Well there's no real weight on the wood yet is there Rodney? and off they would go, these lads were really earning there brass.

I was getting another five or six inches out of the right-hand side and it was like chiselling Weetabix. Then all of a sudden, without much of a to-do and not much noise, a bloody big piece flit off the side, like. Christ! I thought, that's excessive bloody pressure from above!

I'm stroking my chin. The other fella's gone white, and then [boom] another piece has come off. Bollocks, we're no longer in charge; it's coming on its own! Forget the tools, the hammers, the Land Rover, the lot. Run!

I decided to run in the direction opposite to the planned fall and fell over a reinforcing bar, ending up on my back looking at the most horrible sight I've ever seen in my life. The arse end's blowing out of it. How are you going to run away from something thirty-five feet in diameter that's coming down? And I thought it's pointless getting up and running because you might be running the wrong way! The thing to do is watch the top and see what happens, and whichever way the top starts to deviate, you leg it in the opposite direction!

It came straight down for forty feet and settled. Now, when they'd completed it in 1974, they'd put a bloody wooden lid on the top to stop the rain getting at the refractory. The air pressure had built up and blew the bloody lid straight off – and it's heading for Canvey Island town centre like a giant gramophone record! I'm thinking we're in real trouble here.

We're going to look a load of pillocks, I thought, we've been here for three weeks and just reduced it by 40 feet without me striking a match.!

It had had this nasty shock by coming straight down for forty feet, but it must have still been leaning. Then just like slow motion, it fell straight down the bloody middle of all the oil drums that were laid out for us to get it down the middle of. Beautiful, you know.

The funny thing was this young lad, when he'd stopped bloody dithering, he came running and said, "I wanted to come and get you but my legs wouldn't work!" It's like when the devil's chasing you in a dream, it's just like that. But it were real you know.

Anyhow, I got the £12,000 for doing it but it was a great shame that it came down a day early! I'm just happy that no-one got killed.

(And now the other side of the story from Fred's widow, Sheila)

The thing to do is watch the top and see what happens, and whichever way the top starts to deviate you leg it in the opposite direction!

"The bloody thing fell down a day early," said Fred about the Canvey Island Chimney disaster during his after-dinner-talks. I know – I was there. He always told the story with such eloquence, but never mentioned that he almost gave me cardiac arrest on that day with his antics!

"We'll meet you in the pub at dinnertime," he'd said to me that morning. It was almost noon, and setting off from the hotel with Nathan in the back of the car, he quipped, "Mum, I can't see Fred's chimney". Now Canvey Island is flat, and the steel-reinforced, 450ft, concrete chimney weighing almost 2,500 tons was a prominent feature on the skyline. "Nonsense," I said – but still he insisted it was not there.

He was right. The chimney was no more. I sped off towards the demolition site, nearly mowing down an old woman pushing a shopping trolley, and got to the perimeter of the site to see a cloud of dust rising from the ground in the distance like some evil apparition. Glum-faced demolition workers, who told me the chimney had accidentally collapsed, met me at the gates. I feared the worst; I thought Fred would be dead, I knew his team of men would have been working on it when it fell.

It was always Fred's manner to laugh things off in public. However, in private I knew how disturbed he had been by the incident. He blamed it on interference from the 'health and safety' men, undermining his confidence by carrying out tests on his wooden telegraph poles. Educated men, with new rigger boots and shiny hard hats, (as he put it), were to blame for not letting him get on with a job he had successfully done since being a young man.

Fred was in shock, and it took him several months to come to terms with what had happened at Canvey Island. Nevertheless, like the tough man he was, it did not deter him from future chimney-felling jobs, as we all know. Right up to six months before he sadly left us for a place much higher than a chimney, he was still knocking 'em down with gusto.

Before I could ask about possible fatalities, a beaming Fred came sauntering over to the car looking like a naughty little boy caught out. "Aye, well – nobody's been killed, but it's bloody knackered up their fancy day tomorrow, like." He grinned at me, "Fell down a day early!"

...Aye, well – nobody's been killed, but it's bloody knackered up their fancy day tomorrow, like. He grinned at me, Fell down a day early ....

Fred saw the funny side, he said. However, in the pub later that night, badly shaken, he told the tale of how he ran away as the job went out of control and how he'd tripped over a steel reinforcing bar, only to watch the concrete giant waver only yards away from where he lay. He and his team could have been killed. His thoughts as he ran centred on the men helping him. Had they escaped in time? It was potentially the most disastrous chimney in his thirty-year career as a steeplejack. Fred expanded the tale to the gathered group, and told them that he had nibbled out about six inches too much from the cut in the base of the chimney. That had caused the weight to disperse unevenly, and thus caused stress lines in the concrete, resulting in the eventual collapse.

A mere speck at the top of the steeple, Mr Dibnah goes to work on demolition.

THE LAST OF A LOCAL LANDMARK

STARTING at the top is sometimes the recipe for success but for Fred Dibnah it is a necessity that spells the end for St. John's Church.

The 150ft steeple, which has towered above Radcliffe New Road for more than a century, is the last major part of the church to be demolished. The main body lies in rubble already and the spire will soon follow.

The man with the best view of the situation is steeplejack Fred Dibnah. He has seen many great pieces of architecture fall but he is still sad at the loss of a building like St. John's

Church. He works alone at the top throwing down the stone piece by piece.

The 28 cwt cast-steel bell is still in the spire and Mr Dibnah fears that the stones he drops through will bring it down, but the debris must be dropped on the inside because of the risk of damaging graves.

Chimney climb to danger

POLICE had to coax down a man who diced with death by climbing 250 feet up a mill chimney last night.

The young man, who has not been named, scrambled in his stocking feet up ladders which had been fixed to Darwen's 320 feet high India Mill chimney by Bolton steeplejack Fred Dibnah.

The distressed man, who is thought to have had a domestic dispute, was persuaded by police to inch his way down the icy rungs as horrified onlookers watched.

He is being treated in hospital.

Fred had strung his chain of ladders to the top of the town's famous landmark for a charity stunt last weekend. But it had to be called off because of high winds.

Fred's lovebird rescue mission

By JENNIFER BRADBURY

STEEPLEJACK-cum-television raconteur Fred Dibnah took a step back in time yesterday when he returned to climb his first-ever chimney.

The opportunity to rescale the 262ft Barrow Bridge chimney came about because the RSPB is trying to encourage a pair of rare peregrine falcons to set up nest in a safe haven.

The love birds were found breeding recently on an industrial site and the RSPB were keen to find the birds safe alternative accommodation.

Nesting

And so Fred was sent on his mission to scale the heights of the chimney and install a specially built nesting box, pictured, - which the birds will hopefully come to view as their home.

The man who reunited Fred with his first chimney is Tony Johnson, Bolton's RSPB group leader.

He explained that the birds had been spotted in the Barrow Bridge area and it was highly likely that they had been prospecting the chimney as a nest.

"Fred is working on the chimney for the next couple of months so it's unlikely they will nest this year.

"But fingers crossed that they build a home in the chimney next year.

"The birds are extremely rare and so very important. Twenty years ago they were nearly wiped out by DDT poisoning. "Because they are rare it is highly important that their nesting site is safe because there are some unscrupulous people out there who would steal their eggs or their young."

● Back up to the crow's nest goes Dibnah . . . but it's not just another bird's eye view!

IN YOUR VIEW — AND MINE

FRED IS TV'S MOST UNLIKELY STAR

AN unlikely star emerged from your letters last week. It's surprising because he's just an ordinary bloke — and in a repeat series late on Sunday nights. But Fred Dibnah, the Bolton steeplejack, seems to have captured your imaginations.

● Reminds me of my father who travelled the home countries as a steeplejack. Unlike Mr Dibnah, he'd no other interests, but worked at this hard and dangerous job until he was 82. — Mrs J. Fraser, 15-2 Hutchison Loan, Edinburgh.

● Such a down-to-earth person for a steeplejack! I admire the way his wife gets involved in all his projects. — Mrs M. Petty, 42 Kennedy Gdns., Billingham.

● What a variety of work Fred does. He's a real jack of all trades. I look forward to the rest of this excellent series. — Freda Anderson, 14 Priory Green, Newcastle.

Fred tells me he's still climbing chimneys and playing with steam engines. He was on his way to Carnforth Railway Museum with wife Alison to look at the engines when we spoke.

He says he's had more letters than ever with the TV repeats. "A new show tacked on to this series will show a great big chimney coming down—better than the one they show every week," he says.

The Dibnah's have three daughters, Jane (14), Lorna (12) and Caroline (5).

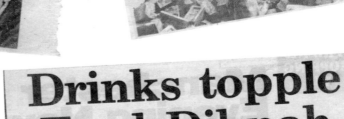

Drinks topple Fred Dibnah

By Patricia Roberts

STEEPLEJACK and TV personality Fred Dibnah celebrated rather too well after successfully demolishing yet another chimney, Bolton magistrates were told today.

And it cost him his driving licence for 12 months when the court heard that he was more than twice above the legal blood-alcohol limit when stopped by police.

Dibnah, aged 50, of Radcliffe Road, Bolton, admitted driving with an excess of alcohol in his blood. He was fined £200 and ordered to pay £25 costs. He also

admitted speeding and was fined £25.

Mr Peter Cave, prosecuting, said that Dibnah was spotted by a policeman on Manchester Road, Bolton, on June 23 driving a Land-Rover between 46 and 48 mph.

When he was stopped the policeman thought his breath smelt of alcohol. Tests showed he had 72 micrograms of alcohol per 100 mls of blood.

Mr Brendan Hegerty, defending, said that on the day of the

offence Dibnah had been working in Liverpool demolishing a chimney.

His was a difficult and dangerous job which put great strain on the individuals involved. It had taken many days of hard work to prepare the chimney.

The chimney was demolished without any problems and afterwards Dibnah and his team celebrated "a little too well" to release the tensions

Mr Hegerty said Dibnah had held a clean licence for many years and fully appreciated the foolishness of what had happened

Fred Dibnah

Always in the Papers

by Sheila Dibnah

BIG chimneys

MR. F. DIBNAH, whose home address is 8 Alfred-st. (near Burnden Park), writes to us from Germany, where he is at present doing his National Service, asking for some details about chimneys.

Hardly surprising that he should ask about chimneys for he is a steeplejack in civil life! Mr. Dibnah writes: "Can you tell me something about some old chimneys, such as Dobson's, or the one at Barrow Bridge?"

He also asks did Bolton ever have the biggest chimney in the country. So far as can be traced we never had the country's biggest chimney, but for many years the tallest stack in Lancashire was at Dobson and Barlow's Kay-st. works—367½ft high. For years people argued that it's height was 369½ft. Then Joe Smith, a local steeplejack, climbed up with a tape-measure! After hours of patient measuring he came to earth to announce that the height was exactly 367½ft—and that was that!

Barrow Bridge chimney was formerly 306ft in height, but in 1929 it was reduced to 288ft. Then in 1945 a crack appeared in the fabric so another 36ft. was taken off, making the chimney a mere 252ft.

Where else could you find such an unlikely celebrity as Fred Dibnah? What was his broad appeal? Certainly he was a walking encyclopaedia on Britain's industrial heritage, not to mention all aspects of engineering and steam – but what was the magic formula that kept us glued to the box whenever he was on? Why did we love to see him standing at the side of a grimy factory chimney with a mad grin on his face, turning to the camera, chirping, "Did yer like that?"

Fred's ultimate goal as a young man was to mend the town hall clock in Bolton, and at the age of 25 he had achieved it. Then the television people came along and catapulted him to fame, and, perhaps as he always maintained, cost him his marriage, the breakdown of which greatly hurt him.

It is surely not surprising that Joanna Kozubska approached Fred in 1996 for an interview for a book called 'The 7 Keys of Charisma' that she was writing. What might have been surprising was to read a passage in the book in which our hero says he often felt a failure. But although he was a natural-born orator, Fred was also sensitive in many ways, and it was this sensitivity and passion for what he believed in that made him real to the viewing public.

The media loved Fred. So open, honest and sincere, nothing would be 'off-limits'. Which other celebrity would tell a reporter all about emotional and financial problems, then add, "Eh, yer won't put all that down, will yer?" It was so typical of him, and, as his national fame and popularity grew, fans would identify with the iconic Fred because of this openness.

Somehow, despite his talent as an intuitive engineer, artist, demolition and steam expert, television celebrity and all round larger-than-life character, he still managed to retain his 'ordinary bloke' appeal. He could have been your granddad, or the bloke next door who you see down the pub on a Friday night.

You never read anything bad about Fred in the newspapers. He lived life in his own way, and did not mind sharing it. He saw nothing wrong in baring his soul.

So what was the 'magic formula' that endeared him to so many, many people? There wasn't one – Fred Dibnah was simply… 'one of us'.

■ Pride before the fall: Fred with one he didn't blow up

Wind damaged cross is hauled down

Bolton steeplejack Fred Dibnah with the unenviable job of removing the cross from the church tower.

A LANDMARK in the Tonge Fold area of Bolton for the past 35 years was taken down today.

For the metal cross on top of St Chad's Church was dislodged by high winds at the week-end. One arm of the cross was broken off.

Firemen were called out by the vicar, the Rev Colin Shaw, after the cross was seen hanging precariously down the side of the church's 70ft tower.

Steeplejack

Part of the footpath below was roped off after firemen checked the cross. Today a steeplejack was working on the tower to remove it.

The cross, which was erected with the church in 1939, was illuminated until the past few years, when maintenance and replacement costs proved prohibitive.

Said Mr Shaw: "I don't think it will be put back up now. Even though it is ornamental, it is too expensive to illuminate it or replace parts."

Blast it! Fred drops bricks a day early

By Roger Williams

BRITAIN'S best-known steeplejack Fred Dibnah has blown his latest project.

TV crews and photographers were invited to watch the Bolton blaster drop a 450ft chimney at Canvey Island, Essex, today.

But 57-year-old Fred went "a tiny bit too far" as he prepared the base and the whole lot fell down 23 hours early.

Only other workers on the former oil refinery site were there to see the concrete chimney's sudden collapse.

After the job was suddenly over Fred said: "It was my decision whether to nibble a bit more out of it or not. It's not a precise science and we went a tiny bit too far. This is the first time we have ever lost one."

The chimney was on the site of a new Safeway store, due to open next month.

Gordon Wotherspoon, Safeway managing director for property, said: "We are all pleased that no injuries were caused and the end result was achieved — albeit a day early.

"Personally, my sympathies are with Fred."

Alf Molyneux
A Trip Of
A Lifetime

My name is Alf Molyneux. And I, like many others, have been touched by the spell of Fred Dibnah. In fact it may seem hard to believe, but I had never even seen him on telly before we met, and I never had any interest in steam. All that changed when I was fortunate enough to be introduced to Fred through a friend, while out drinking at a local club.

This is my story of my short time with my great pal, the late Fred Dibnah MBE.

I've worked in the mining industry most of my life, and of course, when Fred and I got chatting in the club, Fred got excited about this and invited me down to see his pithead gear in the yard. While I was doing the grand tour of the place, which took about an hour with him telling me where stuff came from, he says "Can you give us a lift for a bit, mate?" So I did, and that's how it all started, me coming down to the yard from then on.

Eventually, a group of my mates started coming down as well. These were men interested in mining. One Saturday, I'd mentioned that I was going to Fred's yard, and told them about his pithead gear. They all wanted to see it, and so Saturdays became a regular day for us all to go to Fred's and help out wherever we could. Saturdays at the yard became like open house, and people would wander in to meet him. Fred had time for them all.

My mate, Jimmy Crooks, and I got a big team together, so we could get stuck in sinking the pit shaft and other jobs that Fred was on with. He wanted to get his mine up and running, and it would have been an authentic replica, actually passing through a coal seam, because the yard is in a mining area, but the idea wasn't to mine coal really, just look as though we were. It would have happened too, but for him passing on. It was his dream to own his own pit.

They were good, enjoyable times because he was a nice sociable chap and I recall when I first met him that some blokes wanted an autograph and Fred spoke to them like he'd known them all his life. That's how he was, you see, right friendly, like. I never knew him to refuse an autograph, photograph or chance of a chat, he'd talk to anyone.

But he was serious about work. The work we did with him on various projects was always carried out in the old-fashioned way. Even if it was easier and quicker to do it the modern way, he wouldn't have any of it.

I went with Fred to his last but one chimney drop at Brandlesholme, near Bury. It was funny really, because he asked me to go with him when he was sorting out the contract part. I said I didn't know 'owt about dropping chimneys but he goes "Naah, mate - you look the part!" So I kept nodding and smiling while he talked to the gaffer. When he'd got the job, I went with him on the first day, and worked alongside him for a couple of hours, but I hurt my knee, so that were that - I couldn't go again!

I've always said though, one of the greatest things about meeting Fred was that trip where we went round Britain on the engine. The people we met on the way, and the warmth of them, was a true highlight. The engine was special to me as well, because I gave him a lift with building it, I was involved in a bit of everything. I'm not an engineer, but I did some labouring for Fred, it was more or less assembling everything, really. Various parts hadn't been made such as the throat plate. When he had a new one made, it was X-rayed and found to have cracks in, so we had to have another one done. That held us up a bit. The biggest job I did was the stays which were done by hammer; he wouldn't have them done by rivet gun.

All knocked over, the threaded stays, inside and out, by hand. He's asked me if I were any good at it you see, and I told him I'd never done any, so he showed me, like, and did one himself, and I told him I could manage that. It was a noisy job though, many thousands of hammer blows, especially the inside ones - you come out and you are deaf! Took me many weeks, but he was happy with what I had done.

I can't remember the exact date when he told me he'd got cancer; I had only known him a spell before that. He just wanted to carry on basically; they'd given him about twelve months. Fred just said to me one day, "We are doing this series, like, and you are coming!" I told him my wife, Wendy, might not be keen on being on her own at night, but Fred didn't take any notice. We were right on the last minute because of working on the mineshaft, but we completed the engine in time for this epic journey.

The director would say, "We'll not be filming on Monday, Fred's not so good but come down to the yard just in case". Then Fred would appear, seemingly as fit as a fiddle, and say, "Are we ready for off then, or what?". Just like that. He wanted to press on, there were no stopping him, he was determined. It happened more than once. He was very ill by then, but was still as friendly with everybody.

The engine became his passion, and the wonderful trip we did spurred him on. My job was steersman. I'd had no experience, but I did all right, I suppose, especially once the steering chains were shortened, which made the job a lot easier. I remember coming down Llanberris Pass, Gwynedd in North Wales, a beautiful location, my favourite as well was around the Peak District, those long drives.

It was something Fred had always wanted to do, drive around the country on his engine, Betsy, and I was honoured to be a part of it. We had a few teething troubles at first, but they got sorted out. Anyway, end of the day, there were no real problems and it was the experience of a lifetime for us both.

Fred Meets the Queen
By Sheila Dibnah

The Beatles were number one in the 'pop charts', the summer hot, and I was just seven years old and growing up in 1960s Bolton. The Queen was coming to town, and all us school pupils traipsed off at playtime to see her pass by the end of the road. I often wonder nowadays if Fred had heard she was coming to town that day. Being a bit of a royalist, maybe he, too, was in the crowd. On the other hand, perhaps he would be more than likely to be stuck up a ladder, mending a chimney somewhere in his hometown? In any case, it would be over 40 years before fate would again assemble the three of us in the same place, but this time under one roof. A particularly fine roof, too – Buckingham Palace!

We set off for London on a warm, early July day in 2004. Over previous months we had received several letters from the Palace, but the first one prompted a typical response from Fred: "Some bugger's 'avin me on. Who'd give a bloody gong to a daft pillock like me?" (Shortly afterwards he repeated the sentiment in his engine shed as he held a cup of coffee, shaking his head in disbelief at the picture of the Queen and Prince Phillip on the wall of the shed!). Left to Fred, the letters would have gone unanswered – it was only when I replied and we got a firm date arranged that he started taking the matter seriously.

Now here it was, the appointed day – July 7th. We were in a room of a hotel near Buckingham Palace, preparing to meet Her Majesty. We had travelled down to London from Bolton the previous day and I was brushing Fred's jacket as he dressed for the most important occasion of his life. It was the first time I had ever seen him nervous, but he was still cracking jokes. "Should have come down with me bloody roller, cock: if Her Majesty could have thrown me a few bags of coal on, I could have flattened the gravel at the palace by Royal Appointment. Can you imagine the steam men if I had a royal crest on the side of me engine that said "Fred Dibnah by Royal Appointment"? That would get em talking eh?"

I had hired for Fred a lovely, dark morning suit, complete with cream waistcoat and cravat, all set off with a fine top hat. He studied and fiddled with the outfit, particularly the trousers. "Who the bloody hell designs these daft things, eh? There's no belt loop, how can you keep the buggers up?"

I showed him the adjustable waistband.

"What the hell good is that with the size of my beer belly? I'll end up exposing me wedding tackle to the Queen of England if I'm not careful!" He also moaned about not being able to keep the top hat straight on his head, but stuffing it with a previous day's newspaper soon solved that problem. But the trousers presented a bit more of a dilemma. He had an idea that he only explained later... "Aye, well, some time ago – I'd made me own braces in me shed out of some dog-clips and bits of old string. I don't like them modern ones they make these days, no good when you are doing 'owt a bit strenuous, like. The old ones were better in the days when you had buttons on your trousers, but you can't get them now, it's like owt else, but these home-made braces do the trick. You just hook 'em through your belt loops. Anyway, that particular morning, standing there getting ready to meet the Queen, there were 'nowt else for it but use the ones I'd made. So I punched bloody great holes in these posh pants with a fork we'd nicked from the hotel, and shoved the dog clips through. The missus weren't too keen on me going to meet the Queen of England with me pants held up with string, but it worked all right. Anyway, no bugger knew, so I don't know what she were on about!"

Fred and I left the hotel and walked to the palace gates with sons, Jack and Roger. David Hall was there with his film crew, preserving the occasion for posterity, and we stopped and chatted for a while. It was blowing a gale, and Fred held on to his top hat while my floaty dress whipped around my legs. Soon it was time to go through the gates and walk over the gravelled forecourt toward the famous building. Entering the palace, we were met by a polite, well-groomed usher, who told us to proceed up a massive, rococo-style gold staircase. What an awesome, magical feeling as we saw the 'old masters' lining the walls! This was it – inside the palace!

At the top of the stairs, Fred was instructed to go into a side room, while the boys and I were escorted into the elaborate ballroom used for state functions. A band located high on a decorative gallery played 'old standards' as we waited and looked around the room, taking in the sea of colourful hats and 'posh frocks' as Fred would call them.

Later, I asked, "What did she say to you then, Fred?" The Queen, it seems, after intimating that she always watched and liked his programmes, had said, "Are you still knocking down factory chimneys, Mr Dibnah?" And he had replied, "Yeah yer Majesty, I've got a big mortgage to pay, so I can't give up just yet – and besides, I like it!" She smiled and shook his hand after the brief exchange.

Obviously, it was a great honour meeting the Queen, and Fred was chuffed to bits that she loved all his programmes. However, the most heart-warming part was that as a working class man, he had made it to Buckingham Palace, all the way from his humble background, something that would have made his mother proud, as revealed in his comments later – "I wish me mam could have seen it, she'd have been reet proud of me. She always wanted me to have an office job when I was younger. I wish she'd seen her Freddie in London. She'd have told all her mates down at the gasworks where she worked … she'd have been reet proud an' all."

Eventually, we stood as the Queen, resplendent in a lime green outfit with a huge diamond brooch, entered to our left. She was accompanied by liveried guards and proceeded to the front of the ballroom, where a long table covered in thick damask carried the awards on small, plump cushions.

A fanfare of trumpets blared and the ceremony began. We watched as worthy people from all walks of life received knighthoods, OBEs and MBEs. Then it was Fred's turn. "Doctor Frederick Dibnah, for services to television and broadcasting", the cut-glass voice of the announcer proclaimed over the public address system. Fred entered the room and briefly bowed in front of the Queen. A short exchange took place, and I saw Fred lean forward and cup his hand to his good ear. I can just imagine it – "Yer wot, cock – you'll have to speak up a bit, I'm deaf!" The Queen pinned the medal on Fred; he bowed again and left the room.

The ceremony continued for about two hours, and finally we rose to the National Anthem as the Queen left the room. I noticed her piercing blue eyes as she looked directly at us.

Deuce!

Two greats. Fred Dibnah MBE and Tennis star Tim Henman OBE.
Enjoying their medals at Buckingham Palace

My Time With Fred A Much-Missed Pal!

By Neil Carney

I served an apprenticeship in mechanical engineering as a fitter and turner in Liverpool and joined the Lancashire Traction Engine club in 1965 when it was quite new.

I first met Fred Dibnah at one of the early traction engine rallies at Burtonwood in the late 1960s. He had recently bought his steam roller, (later named 'Betsy' after his mother), and had embarked on the long task of completely rebuilding it, including a new boiler, which he made himself. To do this, Fred consulted retired boiler makers and acquired all the necessary tools. He must have been an ideal student because with Fred it was once shown, never forgotten.

A steam boiler has to be inspected at regular stages during the construction, so the workmanship has to be of the highest standard. Fred's was a riveted construction - he never became a welder- no certificates for our Fred!

I kept in touch with Fred during the rebuild, but did not actually play any part in it. He worked under a tarpaulin slung between the trees in his back garden in the early days. He did eventually build a substantial shed which grew over the years to become the "Victorian Factory" that we know today.

I took early retirement in 1989 and Fred got to hear of this. He was without a mate at that time and was overhauling a steam engine for Gwynedd Council. The Council intended to put the engine back into use as an attraction at a craft centre they were developing at Parc Glynllifon, South Carnarvon in Wales. Fred asked me if I would help him build the engine. This was a job that suited me fine, as we were to work, Monday to Friday, in Wales for about three months. We finally left the engine in working order, driven by a boiler which we installed, donated by a local bakery,.

I continued with Fred on the steeplejacking side of his work, during a five year period, 1989-1994. Our time together was more or less divided between steeplejacking and "playing in't garden" as he would put it. This involved working on any of his 14 machines, all driven from his steam-driven line shafting. His beautiful little yard engine called Caroline started its life driving a mechanical stoker at an old mill – it was made in Bolton!

My involvement with the chimney work consisted of pulling the ladders and decking up to his working level, and supplying any materials or equipment Fred required. I had a lot of free time down below, but I had to be ready if anything was needed upstairs.

It was my job to paint the guttering and downspouts on a small church while Fred pointed the steeple up above me. I was particully proud that I managed to modify the clock at the same church much to the delight of the vicar.

.... I assisted on about 15 chimney drops during my five happy years with Fred. My job was the 'gardening' which involved keeping the working area clean and tidy ....

I assisted on about 15 chimney drops during my five years with Fred. My job was "the gardening", which involved keeping the working area clean and tidy by removing the bricks which were cut from the chimney base. I also cut the props, [usually telegraph poles] to the exact length required. Fred always invited me to do this with his chainsaw and he reckoned I got them more square at the cut than he could, "It's these glasses," he would say when he cut one himself and found it "a bit out"!

When I attended a 'dropping', I was usually required to drive the Land Rover and compressor back home to Radcliffe Road, Bolton. I am not a drinking man myself, and would leave Fred to celebrate a job well done. During my time with Fred the only chimney drop that went wrong was perhaps due to Fred's explanation of how the job was done, in the pub, on the night before. This was at Cockermouth, in Cumbria. Some members of his audience attempted to do the job overnight...but failed! All the props were burned away, but miraculously the chimney stood its ground. At about 5 o'clock in the morning on the day of the drop the police called on us to tell us the tale. Fred and I attended the scene straight away, and managed to put in a few new props. The reason the chimney had not fallen was simply that the "slot" was not fully cut half way. This is a job that is always left until the morning of the drop.

The local Fire Brigade had been called but they would not go near it. The Commander had decided that, there being no danger to life and limb or any property in the vicinity, they would take no risks. It did fall later in the day under Fred's full control after our own fire was lit.

Another strange thing occurred at Whitworth. It was a straightforward job, but when the fire was lit, there appeared to be a strong downdraught in the chimney which caused the fire to burn outside up the brickwork instead of burning through the props. Nothing could be done but hope for a gust of wind in the right direction to turn the flames inside. After about ten anxious minutes, all went well and the chimney duly fell, exactly on line, but a little late!

After leaving Fred in1994, I kept in touch with him to follow the progress with his Aveling Steam Tractor, the one used on his last tour with the BBC. I had but little interest in his mine shaft and I sincerely hoped that it would not take too much of his time off completing his tractor. It would have been a tragedy had he not completed it in time for his tour. However Fred made it, and I am sure that his desire to complete 27 years work extended his life by some two years.

I lost a good friend in Fred; we did not share social time together, but the five years we "worked", if you can call "playing in't garden" work, were most enjoyable. He appreciated my engineering background and I certainly appreciated his practical approach to a problem. Nothing ever got the better of Fred, apart from calculation, (he tended to leave that to me), but had I not been there he would have found some other way of getting a tricky job done.

Fred's MBE was never awarded to a more fitting person; his interests lay in a time when we had an Empire! I don't doubt that, right now, he will be discussing his 'methods' with his mentor, Mr I K Brunel.

I was honoured that Fred had requested that I should drive his steam roller, Betsy, on the day of his funeral. It was a duty that I carried out with precision, respect, and sadness.

Rest in peace

Neil Carney

Doctor Dibnah
By Sheila Dibnah

Two Honorary degrees were awarded to our flat-capped hero: The first was from The Robert Gordon University in Aberdeen, the other from Birmingham University. Both were well deserved. The former went like clockwork – the latter rather hectic at times.

On the outskirts of Birmingham with me at the wheel and Fred giving directions, we headed towards the University campus, confident we were in the right area. Soon, we looked around helplessly – it was obvious we were lost! Fred lifted his cap and scratched his head, puzzling over a map provided by the University, "Why do they always print these bloody things in a foreign language? I can't understand this bugger; which way up is it anyway," He caught sight of a scruffy-looking youth and wound down the window, shouting across the road "Hey up

mate, yer don't know where the University is by any chance do yer?" I cringed, noticing the dirty, hooded top as he approached and beamed a discoloured smile in our direction. "Wow! Solid! Well! Good, mate, you're that bloke off telly arn't you, seen yer on there?" Fred, oblivious as always to imminent danger, quipped "Aye and I'm being given an award in back street mechanicing today and I'm bloody late, do you know the way there an' all?" To my alarm, the youth without warning opened the back door and jumped in, filling the car with a stale reek of cigarettes. Leaning forward between the seats, he offered to take us to the University. I gripped the wheel in terror, as we sallied forth amidst four-lane traffic, ending up at a large roundabout, with me eyeing the youth in the rear-view mirror while Fred gave a lecture about the modern world, but pleased he's been recognised by

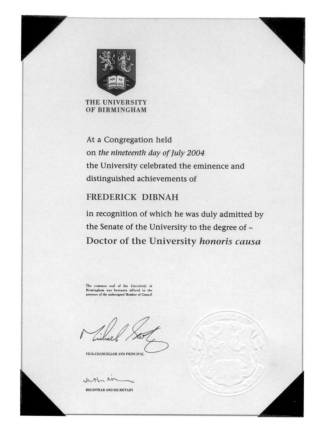

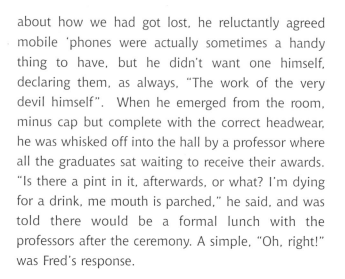

about how we had got lost, he reluctantly agreed mobile 'phones were actually sometimes a handy thing to have, but he didn't want one himself, declaring them, as always, "The work of the very devil himself". When he emerged from the room, minus cap but complete with the correct headwear, he was whisked off into the hall by a professor where all the graduates sat waiting to receive their awards. "Is there a pint in it, afterwards, or what? I'm dying for a drink, me mouth is parched," he said, and was told there would be a formal lunch with the professors after the ceremony. A simple, "Oh, right!" was Fred's response.

I took a seat amongst the large crowd of family and friends of the graduates, waiting until my man came forward to receive his own award. Then his name was announced, and he shuffled forward in that oh-

this young fellow, who seemed to be taking an interest in Fred's large, gold watch chain. I was relieved when a big municipal building came into view, which the youth immediately declared to be the University.

Fred thanked him, and to my relief, the youth disappeared after Fred had hurriedly provided an autograph on a cigarette packet. We parked up, at least grateful we'd now found the University.

….the trouble was, it was the wrong one - there are two in Birmingham!

Eventually, after several phone calls to a number provided on the printed map, we arrived in a fluster at the correct location some forty minutes late, where we were greeted by group of frantic academics eager to proceed with the awards ceremony. Fred was immediately rushed into the robing room to change into formal attire. I was fascinated, and stood close by watching the performance, as Fred quite calmly fitted in with what was required of him and donned a colourful, heavy robe. Giving a running commentary

so-familiar style of his, with a beaming smile worthy of any Oscar award winner. Born a natural showman, he gave a superb acceptance speech and soon had the crowd in stitches with his 'Dibnahisms'.

It went well, and everyone gave him a rapturous round of applause at the end, for they knew they had seen a living legend in action. On return to the robing room, formal photographs were taken, and Fred was offered a drink, but he was more interested in the clock tower on the University campus, and arrangements were made for us to ascend after lunch and take a look at the clock mechanism. I expected the 'formal' afterwards to be a stuffy affair, but that, too, was fun. As I sat between two professors, I wondered how these clever academics might take to Fred's sometimes-colourful language, and soon enough, he began with a tale about some engine driver on the outskirts of Bolton called Ludwig who had been killed when a railway locomotive fell down a disused mineshaft! I watched Fred hold court and light up the table of ten with many of his idiosyncratic tales; he was natural and completely at ease, and delivered each gem of wisdom in his own unique style.

After a steep climb up the clock tower, and some more photographs with the professors, it was nearly time to leave and head back up North. We took away with us some special memories, and I could see it had been a brilliant day for Doctor Dibnah – and everyone else I presume.

Fred's Last Stand

By Sheila Dibnah

"The Story of Fred Dibnah's last chimney drop"

"No wonder they called you a lunatic when you built a chimney on your mum's house as a lad," I moaned at Fred, exasperated at what I was hearing, adding, "They could see you were a stubborn bugger even then!" He'd just told me that he'd undertaken another chimney-felling job at Park Mill in Royton, near Oldham in Lancashire.

Nothing unusual in that, except that this was May 2004 and by this time Fred was extremely poorly after two cycles of chemotherapy and a gruelling work schedule restoring his steam tractor. He knew he hadn't got long left, but was determined not to be stopped by the increasing effects of his illness. I saw the mill chimney as a portent, looming as it did some 200ft up in the sky, and like Fred, awaiting its fate. "You simply can't do it – it'll kill you!" I said, trying to sound firm. But Fred knew it was to be the last time he would fell a factory chimney, and nothing could dissuade him from this one last victory. He had agreed to demolish the stack for an old mate called

Roy Fischer, who he learned was clearing the site for development with smart, new housing.

The mill opened in 1913 during the pre-First World War cotton boom in Lancashire, and went on spinning up until 1977. Fred, uneasy that the "Yuppies were moving in and taking over with their shiny cars and black briefcases with brass corners," as he put it, nevertheless soon set about assembling the usual team of helpers. His main right-hand man, Eddie Chattwood, friend and fellow steeplejack, was the first he called. They had worked together since the late 1960's and Eddie was as wild and tough as Fred, and, although this was a sad occasion, Eddie had no hesitation in accepting this final chance to work alongside his mate. Others were assembled, and amongst them a newcomer to chimney-felling, Fred's pal David Bank-Fear, managing director of Southern Springs, based in Dorset who travelled north for this auspicious occasion.

A chimney-felling takes a week to prepare, with a team of men, supervised by and including Fred, using jigger picks and jack hammers to cut a slot in the base. The red-brick chimney would be several feet thick at the bottom, where Fred and his men would insert telegraph poles to prop up the weight of many tons, ready for burning in the usual fashion.

This truly was a labour of love. Fred was back to his usual self, arranging things, going off to the site in his Land Rover everyday, which was festooned with all the heavy gear the lads would need on a typical felling operation. As always, they'd retire to the pub at lunchtime, Fred in his element, covered in brick dust and soot, calloused hand serially clutching several pints of bitter before heading back on site to tackle the afternoon's heavy work.

On his return home however, I saw the stress and strain in his face, but he tried hard not to show it as I tried to insist that he should let the others do all the work. "What yer mithering on about, woman?" he challenged whenever I grumbled, and I could only wonder at how he managed such arduous work, given his condition.

The day of the felling arrived, and I'd donned a smart lilac jacket with sensible black boots. Fred had asked me to light the chimney fire, since he never lit the fire himself at a chimney felling, being superstitious that something might go wrong if he did. There was a great sense of expectancy as Fred strutted around the chimney, pushing through the crowds to supervise last-minute tasks with his men, showing all the confidence of a 35-year career as a steeplejack. Roger, Fred's youngest son, enchanted the crowd, dressed like a miniature Fred and wearing a top hat, displaying all the charisma of his famous dad and loving every second.

The fire was normally lit around 11.30am and the chimney would crash to earth some 25 to 30 minutes later as the creosote-soaked wood burned away, but on this occasion the crowds had swollen to more than 2,000, so the time was put back to 1pm for the felling, so that everyone could be cleared from the site to a safe distance.

It came at 12.54pm, when the hooter sounded and the structure gradually succumbed to gravity, twisting sickeningly on itself as it fell, close to where Fred was standing. The noise rumbled like thunder, and Fred and the pile of hot bricks were immediately shrouded in a fog of thick dust and soot, from where he finally emerged, holding up his arm in victory, grinning at the crowd. Members of the media came forward, armed with cameras and microphones, requesting Fred to climb up on the brick pile and pose for photos and interviews. This he did, with some obvious effort by now, but nothing would prevent him from enjoying this last conquest. A true showman!

"Did yer like that?" he chirped on request, following it, as always, with what came next – "We're off t'ert pub now, an all!" then set about instructing people how to find the local hostelry.

A police helicopter swirled above us as I took the diesel-soaked, flaming torch and clambered with Fred towards the wood, (also soaked in diesel for easy ignition), that was stacked at the base of the chimney. Sky Television was doing a live broadcast to air; it was the first time in Fred's illustrious career that this had happened, and the large, black camera jostled for a better vantage point among the onlookers. I held the torch close to the wood. "Stick it in thuuur, cock!" Fred instructed, and as soon as I did so, the fire caught hold. Fred instructed everyone to get back, and then stood, as he always did, at the side of the smokestack looking at his pocket watch dangling on the trademark gold chain. He looked at one with the scene, somehow he was peaceful. As the fire raged, cameras clicked, the crowd waited, and Fred, knowing this was his last chimney-felling, looked like an emperor, standing imperiously at the side of his empire waiting for the very last battle to come to a victorious end.

I had often pondered about Fred's liking for drink after a chimney drop. At first, I didn't understand it, but as he explained: "When you've worked on one of them buggers for a week, knowing it could topple and kill yer at any time, yer have to work hard and play hard in my job"

So now it was play time down at the pub. The team of men drank well into the night, surrounded by friends and fans, reminiscing about bygone days and some of the men who had originally built the mills and factory chimneys in Victorian times. Fred added, in a moment of reflection and thoughtfulness, "Yeah mate, you had to be on the wild side and a bit mad to be a steeplejack back then!" At that, he took another long draw on his pint, cheeky smile in place.

Stories to tell, public to entertain, and, as always, the famous 'Peoplejack' had completed another job well on that day.

.... When you've worked on one of them buggers for a week, knowing it could topple and kill yer at any time, yer have to work hard and play hard in my job ....

6th Novemeber 2004
Dr. Fred Dibnah M.B.E. Dies

TV personality and steeplejack Fred Dibnah, 66, has lost his three-year fight against cancer only weeks after filming his final television series.

Bolton-born Mr Dibnah, who became an unlikely celebrity, spurned treatment to tour the UK on a traction engine as part of a 12-part television series.

Fred Dibnah cancelled all appearances and engagements in September after he was taken ill during filming the BBC series "Made in Britain".

He died on Saturday surrounded by friends and family at Bolton Hospice.

The star of over 20 documentaries leaves widow Sheila, brother Graham, step-son Nathan, daughters Jayne Lorner and Caroline, sons Jack & Roger.

Fred's Funeral - A big Day in Bolton
By Paul Donoghue

I kept looking on the internet at the Bolton Evening News site. Fred had died on 6th November 2004 and I wanted to go to the funeral. A few weeks before, I had driven to Manchester on business; once I had had my meeting I got back in the car and drove over to Bolton, I had decided to go to the Hospice and see Fred. I parked outside, next to the trees, looking at the building. I then decided that Fred would be surrounded by close family, and perhaps this wasn't such a good idea. I then drove to Radcliffe Road and stood there looking through the railings at the marvellous sight before me, memories of some great times came back to me, but I cannot describe the sadness in my heart.

The funeral date was announced, it was to be on 16th November 2004. It was to be a public event with everyone invited. I took my black suit to the dry cleaners, to be readied for my attendance.

...... memories of some great times came back to me, but I cannot describe the sadness in my heart.......

On the morning of 16th November I set off for Fred's funeral at 5.30 am. The weather was appalling, it was chucking it down. I had to turn my car round a couple of miles into the journey and go back home for a coat. It was then that I picked up my camera case and put all my equipment in the car. Then I hit the road again, with my wind screen wipers at full pelt all the way.

...... As I looked around I could not believe the number of people who were gathering, women children steam men and friends. ....

I made good time as I travelled the familiar route, and turned into Radcliffe Road at 7am, there were low loaders, steam men and four Traction engines being fettled and polished. The rain just never stopped. It was then that I saw Roy Pinches running around with his new Sony digital video camera. He scurried over to me and gave me a big handshake. He said "I knew you would be here, this is going to be massive, and just about everyone in Lancashire is going to be here." We chatted for 10 minutes and then I left Roy and went to take in the scene. I looked at the flowers hanging on the railings and read some of the little notes of sadness. I could see a lot of activity in the steam sheds. As I looked around I could not believe the number of people who were gathering: women, children, steam men and friends. It was then that I decided to get my camera out and preserve what was fast becoming a film-worthy historical occasion.

I was taken aback by the attention to detail on the trailer that had been especially constructed to carry Fred's coffin. I was impressed that all the tools of a steeplejack were incorporated into the design – ropes, ladders, and pulley's, bosun's chair, chisels and hammers etc. I could see the rollers that had been attached to Fred's ladders so that his coffin would easily slide on and off the trailer. I found out later that the trailer had been designed by long-term friend of Fred's, Michael Webber and that Michael had driven the trailer to Bolton all the way from Worthing on the south coast.

Looking down into the yard, there was smoke and steam bellowing out of the doors. I could see Neil Carney and Fred's youngest son, Roger, getting Fred's roller ready. On the other side of the shed Michael Webber and Jack Dibnah were preparing the newly-completed Aveling and Porter tractor.

The rain was still pouring down, but I honestly don't think the rain was spoiling anything. What gripped you was the crowd, probably 200 people had gathered outside the house, but apart from the hissing of steam engines you could have heard a pin drop.

Suddenly everything went up a gear, the police arrived on motorbikes, and the band of 103 Regiment of the Royal Artillery, Bolton Volunteers, took up their position at the end of Fred's road. The band was going to lead the cortege. Traction engines were making their way down the road ready to take up their position in the procession. Fred's Land Rover suddenly appeared through the gates. The Lanny was in a bit of a state. It was covered in leaves and looked very sad, but someone had made the last-minute decision that the Land Rover should be included in the proceedings. Five minutes later, and after some very quick hosing and cleaning, the Lanny was brought up to scratch and ready to take its rightful place at the rear of Fred's living van, attached with an A frame.

The first engine to steam up the drive was Fred's trusty roller, Betsy, driven by Neil Carney. As the engine pulled on to the road an immaculate black Rolls Royce hearse moved silently next to Michael Webber's trailer. As I looked around I noticed that 10 to 15 news crews had arrived to cover the funeral for local and national television, plus scores of press photographers.

Fred's coffin was gently pulled from the Rolls Royce hearse and then lifted slowly and carefully on to the trailer. The special rollers that had been built in the ladders and the securing mechanism all worked perfectly and Fred was now high above everyone and ready to be paraded one last time in the limelight, in his specially-requested Victorian-style-funeral with steam.

While Fred was being placed on the trailer, Jack Dibnah and Michael Webber made their way slowly up the drive with the beautiful Aveling tractor. They delicately drove the engine to the front of the trailer and hooked it to the rear of the engine.

Everything was almost ready; the police outriders were talking on their radios. The engines were blowing off steam. John Howarth (funeral director) then knocked on the front door and told Fred's widow, Sheila that everyone was ready. As Sheila came out of the house she acknowledged the huge

crowd of onlookers, and then climbed sombrely into a beautiful white vintage Rolls Royce, supported by her son, Nathan, and her mother, Mavis.

A few minutes later the silence was broken by the deafening sound of Betsy's whistle, indicating the start of the procession. I checked my watch, it was exactly 11.15 am. The band started playing sombre music that was fitting for the occasion. Walking up front was the immaculately-dressed John Howarth, funeral director.

The cortège turned on to Bradford Street and then slowly over the St Peters Way Bypass, I will always remember seeing cars stopping on the carriageway and hooting their horns as they spotted Fred's funeral from below. The streets were lined 5 deep. granny's, granddads, mothers, dads, daughters and sons, and toddlers were all stood there with their umbrellas watching this once-in-a-lifetime happening. I saw a full class of infants with their teacher. The teacher was telling the children that Fred Dibnah was a very special man, and to wave as the engines drove past.

As I filmed, it was almost like I was on autopilot. I had been to Bolton many times, but I had never been in Bolton town centre before, but I seemed to instinctively know where the funeral was going and where to point my camera. I had no idea how popular this film was going to become.

As the engines pulled up outside Bolton Parish Church they were greeted by loud applause from the 1000s of people watching. It is a sight I will never forget. Not since the funeral of Princess Diana had I witnessed such scenes.

Outside the church Fred was carefully lowered from the trailer and slowly taken up the steps and along the stone pathway to the church. He was followed by his widow, Sheila and other members of the family. The church was out of bounds to me, so as Fred's service took place I busied myself conducting interviews with the people outside. I heard later that it had been a lovely service and a fitting tribute to our Fred. I did see hundreds of people writing messages of condolence in the entrance to the church.

After a service taking just over an hour, the coffin

came back into view; the applause started again as Fred was lifted back on to the trailer for his final journey to Tong cemetery.

Another deafening whistle from Betsy signalled that everyone was ready to go. A huge plume of smoke and steam engulfed the square outside the church as the engines slackened their brakes and regulators were slowly pushed forward.

The band had completed their duty and dispersed; it was now Betsy that would lead the way. I took up a vantage spot 200 yards away, and as the cortège got closer the applause and whistles from the crowd got louder and louder. I could hear people shouting, "God bless you Fred", "Rest in Peace, Fred", people were truly mourning the loss of a great character.

Everyone involved in the funeral (who I have spoken to) has mentioned when the cortège went past Bolton fire station. I had to stop filming because I was trapped by the crowds. But the story goes that all the firemen and women on duty that day were standing outside the fire station in the pouring rain at the side of their appliances in full dress uniform, saluting Fred's coffin as the funeral drove past. I am grateful to David Jack who seems to have been the only person there with a camera to capture a remarkable photo.

While the funeral made its way around the town, I made my way on foot to Tong cemetery. I was soaked to the skin. The streets were still lined with 1000s of people. I took up position near the gates of the cemetery as the cortège came towards me. I noticed that Betsy was no longer leading the engines. I was told later that she had returned to the sheds at Radcliffe Road, after doing her duty. The real reason was that her tubes were leaking and that she could not get up enough steam to continue.

The ground around the grave was very slippery; hundreds of mourners were gathered around the area to see Fred finally laid to rest. As the engines got nearer I noticed John Howarth (funeral director) riding on the rear of Fred's Aveling tractor as the cortège came to a final halt just 30 yards from the grave.

Fred was moved one last time from the trailer and

slowly carried to his grave. The flat cap that had adorned the coffin was removed and Fred was placed in his final resting place. Almost immediately the whistles on all the traction engines saluted one of the finest gentlemen this country has ever known. I could see tears streaming down the faces of many who were present.

One of the things that has not been made public is that after the funeral, when the crowds had dispersed, Fred's sons, Jack and Roger, drove the Aveling tractor past their Dad's grave; they paused for a while in reflection and then gave a final short blast on the whistle as a final goodbye gesture. The lads then drove past the thousands of graves as they made their way back to Fred's yard.

I drove home again after saying goodbye to all my friends. It was a journey of reflection and sadness. I liked Fred, and his passing was a deep personal loss for me. I returned to Fred's grave a few weeks later on Boxing Day. It was then while the grave was covered in snow that I finally had a chance to pay my respects.

Remembering Fred Dibnah

NOW ONLY £9.99

The DVD everyones talking about
What the television cameras never captured...

REMEMBERING FRED DIBNAH

A tribute to one of Great Britain's most famous and best loved characters

With Special Features

REMEMBERING FRED DIBNAH

A tribute to one of Great Britain's most famous and best loved characters

Rallyscene excellence in production

DVD VIDEO

Digitally Re-mastered

Endorsed by Fred's Widow
Sheila Dibnah

Single DVD - £9.99
Plus £1.50 U.K. Postage & Packing

Special features:
Wetheriggs Steam Plant
Beer Talk (Fred with a pint)
A Tribute from Friends

This programme was originally filmed in the early days when Fred was still working as a Steeplejack, climbing up, and knocking down chimneys.

Our Filming started shortly after Fred's hit BBC 2 series "A year with Fred", and was the first professional video Fred made. This film has now been digitally re-mastered and includs a rare and previously unheard voice-over, where Fred talks us through the film in his own words.

The Day That Bolton Stood Still "A Victorian Funeral with Steam"
Fred Dibnah's funeral procession was one of the biggest events that the people of Bolton and Lancashire have ever seen. The town centre streets were lined three and four deep as this "Son of Bolton", with his oily cap set proudly on top of his coffin, made its way through the streets, being pulled by his own treasured steam tractor and well decorated trailer.

The Day that Bolton stood still is a respectful and dignified film of the Funeral of Fred Dibnah, the film captures all that the television cameras missed and is an historic record of an extraordinary day.

Narration is by Fred's old and treasured friend Neil Carney

www.freddibnah.tv   Order your goods. On-line   By Phone   or by Post

RALLYSCENE
The Pond House,
59 Rotherham Road,
Clowne, Derbyshire,
S43 4PT

Rallyscene™
excellence in production

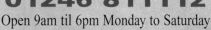
We accept all major Credit & Debit Cards.
Please make cheques payable to Rallyscene
01246 811112
Open 9am til 6pm Monday to Saturday

If you live outside the U.K. please phone to find out the postage rates for your country

Moving the Engines
By Michael Webber

By December 2006 Fred had been departed for more than two years, but still matters regarding his belongings were unresolved. His house, garden and the engines lay still. The old ever-present smells of creosote, oil and smoke had faded away and the ground where once feverish activities were undertaken was now green with vegetation.

One day I received a telephone call of some urgency from Fred's friend, Alan McEwen. He told me that Fred's house had been broken into. I was in Bolton a great deal at this time around then, so I went along to see Sheila. The house had been thoroughly ransacked. I noticed at a passing glance that the garden and engine sheds appeared unaltered. However, once I went in the sheds I immediately noticed that a number of items had been removed from the roller and Fred's tractor. After a police investigation and publicity in the papers, things appeared to settle down a little, so I returned to my home down south for a week or so before coming back to Bolton to spend the Christmas holiday with family.

As many of the shed windows as were practical to board up had been so treated by Alf Molynuex. The doors were secured with wood screws to keep the thieves out. It all had little effect however, as the intruders later ripped a few planks off the wall of a shed or made a hole in the roof to break in. I noticed a pattern emerging, with the thieves returning and taking mostly brass and copper. They threw it down the steep bank near the river at night and probably collected it during the day, undisturbed as they would be about 100 yards away from the house. Copper pipes from the tractor and the big Danks boiler had gone, as had the water and pressure gauges. All of Fred's treasured bronze manufactures and trades plates had gone from the walls of the sheds.

On December 23rd I found the copper top from the tractor on the river bank, and the copper pipes from the roller drain cocks had been ripped off and left there too.

That night I didn't sleep much as I lay awake thinking of what could I do to help.

I thought of all the things in Fred's sheds that had probably gone for scrap. A few months before this, my good friend Michael List Brain from Preston Services had made an inventory for probate of valuables within the sheds. I remember showing Michael some of Fred's part-built, beautifully-made weathervanes. Some of these had been stolen.
There was a dismantled Greens Economiser engine, the bearings and other bronze parts being stolen. The old railway engine whistle that Fred used on the roller, along with boxfull after boxfull of boiler fittings of every description were missing as well. Thousands of pounds worth of items, not to mention the hard graft and sentimental value attached to all these things.

I decided I must do my best to get the Aveling steam roller and 'new' tractor moved away from their home of many years. I had a secret dread of the day those engines had to leave Bolton. Fred's passing was a terrible blow, but for the engines to leave their home was equally hard to accept. I was thinking of all the wonderful times spent with Fred on the roller. The pleasure he had given to millions of people throughout the world with his television programmes. I decided it was my duty to my late friend to put the safety of those precious engines first, and I would just have to face up to any repercussions that my actions caused later.

By the morning of Christmas Eve I had succeeded in gaining help to move the engines. Sheila was of the impression that all must be done to protect Fred's engines, and gave her full approval for me to organize their removal. She was very sad that such drastic action needed to be taken, exclaiming that the engines had been 'born' there, but agreed they were in mortal danger and now needed to be removed for safety. We all knew Fred had made it clear that he always wanted the engines to be based at the yard, and this was the particularly-upsetting part.

There was also the question of Fred's Last Will and Testament to consider since everything was 'frozen' due to legal reasons and nothing could be moved without the Executor's permission. I had to ring Fred's executor to see the lay of the land. He made me aware that what I proposed to do was illegal and it could be perceived that I was stealing Fred's engines. He would rather wait till solicitors could decide what should be done, he said.

The idea of waiting for instructions from solicitors seemed nonsense to me. It would be at least a week before their offices re-opened in the New Year. By that time, the engines might be badly damaged.

I made the decision that I was going to steal Fred's engines and bugger the consequences!

Fred's original transport man, Alan Atkinson, agreed to move and store the two engines at his works in Preston. He sought the help of John Johnson of Banks, near Southport, who are experts in moving large objects with winches, pulleys, tractors and cranes. I had known John Johnson, his brother and father from many years ago as members of the Lancashire Traction Engine fraternity. Their Burrell Gold Medal tractor, 'Forester' was well restored and always beautifully presented and was quite a favourite of Fred's, with its small size, economical running and high road speeds. A plan quickly evolved as to the safest and most efficient way to get the engines up to Radcliffe Road and on to Alan's low loader.

There was little time to prepare for the engines' removal. A large branch from the old ash tree had recently fallen across the bottom of the drive. I worked for a few hours cutting up the branches and clearing them away. The next day, Christmas Day, was to be the last day the engines remained in their sheds. For that afternoon I was alone with my thoughts. It was midday and eerily quiet. There were no cars driving on the road, and no pedestrians walking past the top gates. The disturbing sound of the wind rustling through trees and the loud squawks of black crows above prompted me to look beyond the River Tong to the cemetery, towards the spot where Fred is buried. I was all alone with my emotions, surrounded by the lifetime achievements of my friend.

Boxing Day was the day that Fred's engines were to be taken away from Bolton. It's strange the things that crossed my mind during the short drive to Fred's house from my parents' home. What was going to happen seemed unreal without any ceremony and was overwhelmingly depressing for me.

For the short journey out of the grounds the two engines were to be skilfully dragged and pushed by two vehicles owned and operated by John Johnson and his son. I lit a fire in a tin box, so that we all had some means of keeping warm. Alan Atkinson and his family arrived just before 10a.m. There was little time to chat that day, as John and Alan had hours of work ahead of them once the engines left town. The only member of the Dibnah family present that day was Sheila. She was almost successful in hiding her emotions of sadness, joking about all the smoke from the tin box that seemed more of a hindrance than a fire of comfort. But I saw her inner sadness and later, a tear or two as the engines were tethered on the low loader. John and Alan spent some time setting up the low loader, ready to receive both engines in one trip.

Never before had both of Fred's engines been transported on the same low loader.

The geography of Fred's famous garden always commanded great skill in engine driving and steering. The driveway from the road down to the garden was built by Fred shortly after he had moved to Park Cottage with Alison. At the bottom of the drive next to the ancient ash tree is a very sharp bend which then leads to the engine sheds. From this point the Aveling tractor has a straight line to its shed, but the roller always had another sharp manoeuvre to perform.

First to be moved was Fred's Land Rover. It was in a sorry state with leaves and green moss growing all over. The Lanny, as Fred called it, had been left outside in the yard since Fred died and had been left to the elements.

Once the Lanny had been parked on the road our attentions turned to the Aveling tractor. The tractor was pulled out of the shed and then pushed from behind, up the drive and on to Radcliffe Road and then, finally, on to the front end of Alan's low loader.

It was decided that we would move Fred's roller, 'Betsy', using a strap placed around the headstock. The floor in the roller shed is made from railway sleepers. So many years had passed and the heavy roller has reduced some of those sleepers to what now looked like large Cadbury's Flake bars, broken, split and very crumbly. I steered the roller the way I had in the past, as I knew all the hazards in advance. The roller had only to be moved forward a yard or two and then it required full left-hand lock. When the engine is not in steam a useful trick is to get someone to stand on one of the steering chains, hold on to a lamp bracket for their balance and then bounce their weight up and down. This acts like a crude power steering, as to wind the steering lock on and off while the roller is stationary is extremely exhausting work.

It appeared that there was no way the roller could be pulled or steered around the huge ash tree. It had always been possible while the engine was in steam, but this was looking almost impossible. The towing tractor pulling the roller from the headstock had obviously to be round the sharp right-hand corner near the tree. There was no room to get the other vehicle behind the roller to push. The problem being that regardless of any steering, the roller was being dragged towards the tree, taking the corner too soon. Quick-thinking John Johnson set up a single snatch block or pulley around another tree further up the drive on the left hand side. From there the winch

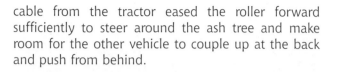

cable from the tractor eased the roller forward sufficiently to steer around the ash tree and make room for the other vehicle to couple up at the back and push from behind.

As the roller was pushed slowly from behind, I wondered if it would ever return home, and how Fred's old house would never be the same without its presence. The roller, I would consider, is the engine most affectionately regarded by Boltonians and Fred's many fans.

The dog-legged manoeuvre, left and right, on to the low loader was considered unwise to attempt. I opted to steer parallel to the low loader then reverse a distance before making the final short distance behind the Aveling tractor. Slowly and steadily the roller was pushed onto the low loader, and then secured for the journey to Preston.

So that was that – for my part the deed was done. A few neighbours and passers-by had started to watch the proceedings. I noticed that a very sad-looking Alf Molyneux had arrived and was talking to Sheila. On the whole, the activity that Boxing Day morning slipped by very quickly and quietly, but strangely unnoticed by the majority as if it never happened.
I could relax a little as Alan and his son attended to securing their precious load to the low loader.

The stolen items I had recovered from down the river bank had already been replaced on the two engines. But there were a number of items belonging to both engines that I was eager for Alan to take with him. From the tractor were the unfinished gear guards and other components, including the usual fire irons, oil cans, tools and just about anything of Fred's that could be crammed into the coal boxes. I had taken off the whistle from the roller a few days earlier as it was a hefty lump of bronze that could so easily have been stolen. This large item was actually a South African Railway chime whistle. Fred had spent a considerable time filing out all the old hammer marks and making a new 'Fred Dibnah style' fancy brass operating lever. As I secured the chime whistle back in its place, Alf busied himself bringing parts from the sheds up to Alan. Fred's Land Rover was pushed into the shed that had housed the Aveling tractor, just before the Johnsons loaded their two vehicles back on to their lorry. By now Alan was just about ready for off. As the two famous engines left their home to an uncertain future, the small group stood watching in silence with their thoughts, as this was most definitely the end of an era for Bolton and the rest of the world.

Eulogy
By Patrick Donoghue

Who was Fred Dibnah? Was he, as he once described himself, "Just a bum who climbs chimneys?" Far from it!

Fred's grandfather, Alfred, left Hull, East Yorkshire, with his wife, Hannah, (née Ford), and crossed the Pennines in 1903 with their young family, settling in Bolton, Lancashire,. Already a trained locksmith, he soon qualified as a 'Master Whitesmith', (someone who makes articles in metals, especially tin). Alfred's son, Frank, married Betsy Travis, and Fred Dibnah was born on April 28, 1938. At that time there were many cotton mills around Bolton, and there is an apocryphal tale that Fred would sit up in his pram to watch the steeplejacks working on the chimneys that dotted the skyline! As a young boy, Fred was often to be found gazing out of his bedroom window, fascinated by the steam locomotives coming and going in the nearby railway yards.

By his own admission, Fred did not shine at school, but certain events during his schoolboy years bear recollection. During the school holidays, Fred would often spend many happy hours at the bleach works where his Dad, Frank, worked. The steam engines and old, (but still efficient), machinery at the works were an endless source of fascination and curiosity for Fred. On one occasion, Fred went with his father, and brother, Graham, on a 'cup tie' special train to Bury when Bolton Wanderers were to play Bury. Fred's principal reason for going was that he wanted to have a train ride over the viaduct at the back of the Dibnah's terraced house, and, rather than go to the football match, he stayed on Bury Station all afternoon, watching the steam locomotives as they arrived and departed.

..... a racing buggy made out of pram wheels, a tea chest and a plank of wood ....

In the early 1960s, Fred's business was a struggle to keep afloat but it was during that decade of Beatles, 'flower power' and Carnaby Street that Fred realised a long-cherished dream: he bought his own steam engine, this for the princely sum of £170! Due to various commitments, it would be 25 years before Fred was satisfied with the result of the restoration project that he undertook, and it was that project together with other 'steam matters' that played a major part in the decision by his first wife, Alison, to end their 17-year marriage. Those "other steam matters" included the purchase and restoration of a stationary steam engine that he used to provide power to a range of machinery in a purpose-built steam workshop at his Radcliffe Road home in Bolton.

It was at the ripe old age of 40, Fred having felled or repaired many chimneys and other tall structures in the interim, that he was 'discovered' by the television camera whilst he was working at the top of Bolton Town Hall. The short 'fill-in' piece at the end of a regional news programme launched a second career which encompassed several highly-popular television series in which Fred was not only involved in steeplejacking but also Britain's heritage – the Industrial Revolution, British monuments and, above all, steam power.

It came to light that Fred had a natural talent for model-making and, encouraged by the school, he entered a four-foot scale model of the Titanic in a competition for schoolboys in Lancashire and Cheshire – Fred won the competition! Not all of his efforts were so successful – a 'racing buggy' made out of pram wheels, a tea chest and a plank of wood, (with brakes designed by Fred), crashed into a Manchester-to-Bolton bus at high speed when the brakes failed! Frank and Betsy Dibnah only learned that Fred had built a two-man canoe in his bedroom when he had to remove the window to get the craft out of the house! But Fred became something of a school celebrity when he was about 13 years of age – the school had been broken into and all the keys stolen. Fred made a complete set of keys for the headmaster, the necessary skill having been learned from his father, who made keys as a hobby.

After a spell at an art school, (Fred had a natural talent in drawing, but none of the teachers could draw, according to him!), Fred started work in a joiner's yard and during his six years there he started up his own steeplejacking business. It was during his two-year National Service period that he first started making the splendid weathercocks which later came to be in considerable demand.

one, we're getting engaged tonight!" They subsequently eloped and were married at Gretna Green! The marriage lasted for 17 years; Fred's second marriage, to Sue, endured for just a handful of years. He later found love with a lovely lass from Blackpool, Sheila, and they were married on September 26, 1998. Not that Fred would ever admit to being a romantic: when he was asked why he had chosen an excerpt from Rachmaninov's Second Piano Concerto to be played when he appeared on Desert Island Discs, the reason he gave was not that it is an utterly romantic piece of music, oh no, not our Fred! He had a friend, he said, who played in the Hallé Orchestra!

It might well be the case that, when Fred's life ended on November 6, 2004, the man with the 'Big Red Book' said: "Fred Dibnah, draughtsman-par-excellence, self-taught engineer-extraordinaire, television personality, keeper of the British heritage flame, perfectionist in all your work, beloved of so many people, heartfelt romantic – This Has Been Your Life. Now please take your cap off before you go any further." And Fred passed through the pearly gates, doffed his cap and spoke that immortal line:

"DID YER LIKE THAT?"

As a result of his television appearances, Fred's natural ability to 'spin a yarn' in a plain, (and sometimes 'earthy'!) manner, brought him into demand as an after-dinner speaker, and one-man stage appearances also came about.

It had become clear right from the start of Fred's emergence into the 'public eye' that, given the option, he disdained the use of modern machinery and methods if the same results could be achieved the 'old-fashioned' way. That approach, and his often- gleeful attitude in using it, endeared him to people, and his passion for the past evoked the element of nostalgia that is present in many of us.

There was, however, another side to Fred that was far removed from chimneys and steeples, steam and tools and oily rags: he was, beneath the bluff exterior, an incurable romantic. He claimed that he first set eyes on his first wife, Alison, when she was walking along a Bolton street while he was at the top of a chimney! Within six weeks he had taken her on an entirely unexpected visit to a jeweller's shop in Manchester. It was only when the jeweller opened a tray of rings that the penny began to drop with Alison, confirmed when Fred, with no declaration of undying love from bended knee, merely said, "Pick

THE STEEPLEJACK.

**A series of photographs from
The Fred Dibnah Heritage Collection**

Classic Tractors

Classic & Vintage Tractors Volume One.

Narrated by keen tractor enthusiast Dr. Busker, this unique video is a must for all those who like vintage and classic tractors. Filmed over several years, all the action is captured from several of England's top tractor events. A host of tractors are featured showing how things were done in years gone by. Featuring names like Hart Parr, Lanz Bulldog, Caterpillar, Fowler, Doe, Fordson and many more.

RUNNING TIME 60 minutes

Only - £7.50

Plus £1.50 U.K. Postage & Packing

Classic & Vintage Tractors Volume Two.

Following on from volume one, this video visits two major tractor events where we get a chance to capture vintage and classic tractors at work. In baking sun we watch a threshing demonstration that shows how corn was harvested and threshed in years gone by. There is also a demonstration of a 1944 Heenan and Froude Dynamometer showing a Titan being put through its paces. Plus we get to see a very rare Alldays Mark II plus a Saunderson Unversal being put through its paces in the ploughing area. Featuring many more exhibits from manufactures John Deere, Olvier, McCormick, Nuffield, International, Caterpillar and many other classic tractors. If you like classic tractors then you'll love this video!

RUNNING TIME 60 minutes

Only - £7.50

Plus £1.50 U.K. Postage & Packing

IDEAL GIFTS

TWO GREAT TRACTOR DVD's

www.freddibnah.tv   Order your goods. On-line   By Phone   or by Post

RALLYSCENE

The Pond House,
59 Rotherham Road,
Clowne, Derbyshire,
S43 4PT

Rallyscene™
excellence in production

VISA EUROCARD MasterCard Maestro SOLO

We accept all major Credit & Debit Cards.
Please make cheques payable to Rallyscene

01246 811112

Open 9am til 6pm Monday to Saturday

If you live outside the U.K. please phone to find out the postage rates for your country

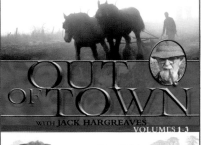
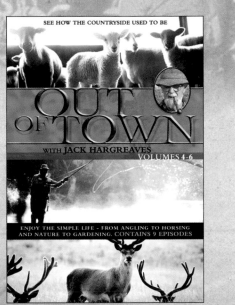
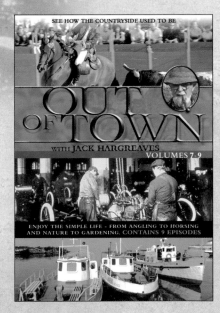 

The Gypsy Collection

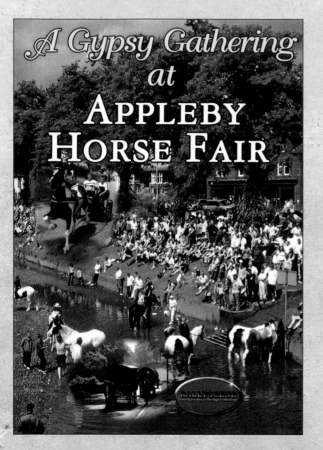

A Gypsy Gathering at APPLEBY HORSE FAIR

A Gypsy Gathering at Appleby Horse Fair.

Everyone is welcome at Appleby Fair. It is one of those rare events where there is no admission fee. You are an invited guest, where you can watch gypsies washing there horses in the River Eden, find horse dealers buying and selling Skewbald and Piebald ponies, see sulkies racing down the lane to Long Marton, or amble along the aisles of the huge market. All the Gypsies in England come to Appleby Horse Fair and bring the sleepy Cumbrian town to life.

If you ever go to Appleby Horse Fair, you will be an invited guest. It's like the aristocracy, the gypsies will be so nice to you, they will treat you with exceptional manners, but you will never be one of them. And as long as you both realise that, you will get along champion.

Features all the action from Appleby Horse Fair, including; living waggons on the road, horse washing in the River Eden, sulky racing on the road to Long Marton, plus very rare film (unseen) footage from Appleby Fair from 1974. **RUNNING TIME 65 minutes approx.**

Now Only
£7.50

Plus £1.50 U.K. Postage & Packing

www.freddibnah.tv

Order your goods. On-line   By Phone   or by Post

RALLYSCENE

The Pond House,
59 Rotherham Road,
Clowne, Derbyshire,
S43 4PT

Rallyscene ™
excellence in production

VISA EUROCARD MasterCard Maestro SOLO

We accept all major Credit & Debit Cards.
Please make cheques payable to Rallyscene

01246 811112
Open 9am til 6pm Monday to Saturday

If you live outside the U.K. please phone to find out the postage rates for your country

The Gypsy Collection

Appleby Horse Fair - The Golden Year.

In this DVD you will witness the town coming alive with the hustle and bustle of gypsies, horses, dealers and tourists all gathered for the selling and racing of horses that is the mainstay of the fair. You will see the sights and sounds of the fair that has a reputation world-wide, attracting visitors and travellers from all over the globe. Watch the horses being prepared and washed in the River Eden, and see an award winning farrier at work. Meet some of the colourful characters who are regulars to the fair, including a special tribute to the late Johnny Eagle.

RUNNING TIME 65 minutes approx.

Now - £7.50
Plus £1.50 U.K.
Postage & Packing

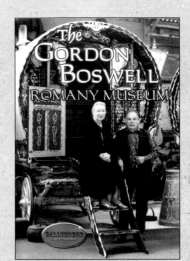

The Gypsies & Horse Dealers at Appleby Horse Fair.

The month of June comes and goes every year, and for gypsies and horse dealers the month of June is everything. It's the only month in the year when the famous Appleby Fair takes place. This video gives you a unique insight of the fair from the comfort of your armchair. From living waggons on the road, to beautiful Piebold and Skewbold horses in the River Eden, there's singing in the pub and trotting horses in the lanes. Deals, wheels, carts and laughter. This is Appleby Horse Fair, once seen, never forgotten.

RUNNING TIME 55 minutes approx.

Now - £7.50
Plus £1.50 U.K.
Postage & Packing

"A Romany Summer" plus "A Family Affair".

In the early 1970's the late Barry Cockcroft made a series of films called "Once in a Lifetime". These programmes were shown on the whole ITV network. One of the more memorable programmes was called "A Romany Summer", which featured a family of Romany Gypsies who travelled and lived on the lanes around York.
This DVD also shows the gypsies at the popular Lee Gap Fair.

RUNNING TIME 50 minutes approx.

Sold under licence to Rallyscene

Now - £7.50
Plus £1.50 U.K.
Postage & Packing

The Gorden Boswell Romany Museum
The Gentleman Gypsy

The Gordon Bosweel Romany Museum is a great experience for all the family, containing one of the countries finest collections of Gypsy Caravans, carts and harnesses in the world.

In this unique film, Gordon Boswell talks about the old Romany way of life (as he guides you through all sections of his museum), his ancestors, and how he came to own one of the most beautiful collections of Gypsy tackle.

RUNNING TIME 1 hour 20 minutes approx.

Only - £7.50
Plus £1.50 U.K.
Postage & Packing

Ballinasloe "The Great Horse Fair".

The Ballinasloe October Horse Fair is famous the world over. It is a place to visit if you want to see the best of Irish bloodstock, and that means the best you will find anywhere in the world. The Great Fair brings to life a unique event. For a few days each year, a quiet County Galway town becomes a maelstrom of wheeling and dealing, of bustle and throng, of songs and stories, as more than three hundred years of tradition and a thousand years of history meet head-on in Europe's greatest frenzy of horse dealing. Narrated by respected horseman Graham Schofield.

RUNNING TIME 55 minutes approx

Now - £7.50
Plus £1.50 U.K.
Postage & Packing

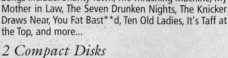
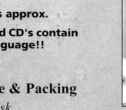
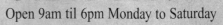